WILD ABOUT
History

WILD ABOUT
History

Written by:
Fiona Macdonald,
John Malam,
Jane Walker

Miles
Kelly

First published in 2018 by Miles Kelly Publishing Ltd
Harding's Barn, Bardfield End Green, Thaxted, Essex, CM6 3PX, UK

2 4 6 8 10 9 7 5 3 1

Publishing Director Belinda Gallagher
Creative Director Jo Cowan
Editorial Director Rosie Neave
Senior Editor Amy Johnson
Cover Designer Joe Jones
Designers Rob Hale, Joe Jones, Andrea Slane
Image Manager Liberty Newton
Indexer Marie Lorimer
Production Elizabeth Collins, Caroline Kelly
Reprographics Stephan Davis, Jennifer Cozens
Assets Lorraine King

Consultants Rupert Matthews, Philip Steele

ISBN 978-1-78617-520-5

Printed in China

British Library Cataloguing-in-Publication Data
A catalogue record for this book is available from the British Library

Made with paper from a sustainable forest

www.mileskelly.net

Contents

ANCIENT EGYPT

1 **Without the river Nile, the civilization of ancient Egypt might never have existed.** The Nile provided water for drinking and watering crops. Every year its floods left a strip of rich, dark soil on both sides of the river where farmers grew crops. The Egyptians called their country *Kemet*, which means 'black land', after this dark soil. The Nile was also a trade route.

▼ The Nile supported many activities such as trade and farming. It was also an important transportation route, with people and goods travelling by boat.

Powerful pharaohs

2 The rulers of ancient Egypt were called pharaohs. The word 'pharaoh' means great house. The pharaoh was the most important and powerful person in the country. Many people believed he was a god.

I DON'T BELIEVE IT!
On special occasions, women wore hair cones made of animal fat scented with spices and herbs. The fat melted, trickling down their heads, making their hair smell sweet but greasy!

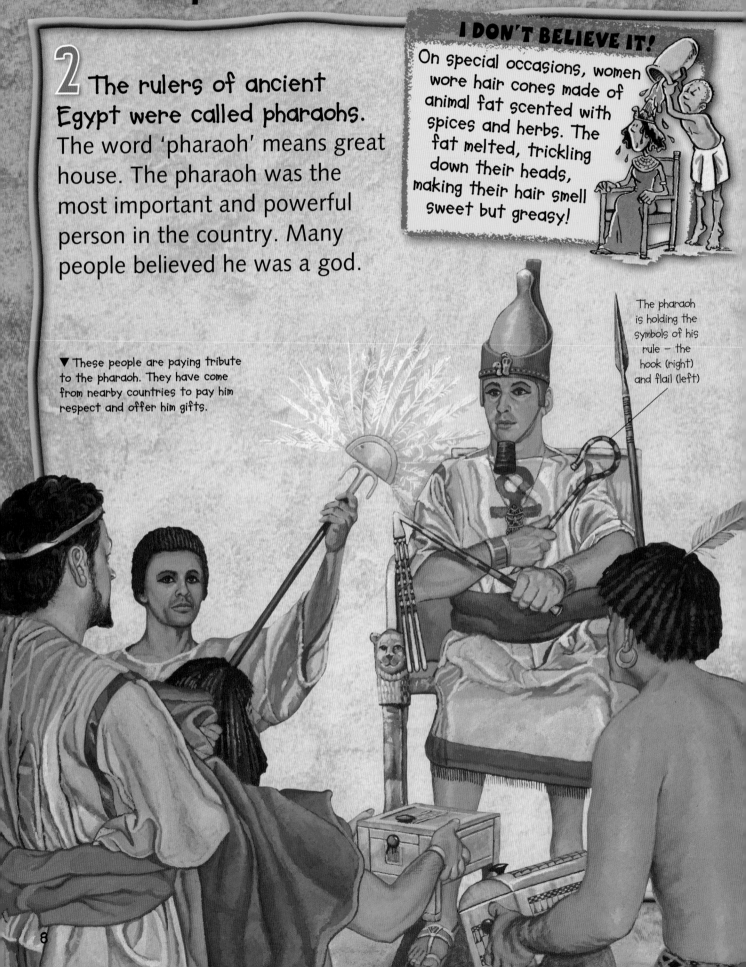

▼ These people are paying tribute to the pharaoh. They have come from nearby countries to pay him respect and offer him gifts.

The pharaoh is holding the symbols of his rule – the hook (right) and flail (left)

◀ On her wedding day, the bride wore a long linen dress or tunic.

3 The pharaoh often married a close female relative, such as his sister or half-sister. In this way the blood of the royal family remained pure. The title of 'pharaoh' was usually passed on to the eldest son of the pharaoh's most important wife.

▲ At Abu Simbel Rameses II built four statues of himself, each over 20 metres tall.

4 Rameses II ruled for more than 60 years. He was the only pharaoh to carry the title 'the Great' after his name. Rameses was a great builder and brave soldier. He was also the father of a large number of children – 96 boys and 60 girls.

A civilization begins

5 More than 7000 years ago, people from Syria and the Sahara moved into Egypt. They learned how to farm crops, and settled in villages along the banks of the Nile and the Nile Delta. By about 5500 years ago, there were two kingdoms, Upper Egypt and Lower Egypt.

6 The history of ancient Egypt began more than 5000 years ago. The first period was called the Old Kingdom, when the Egyptians built the Great Pyramids. Next came the Middle Kingdom and finally the New Kingdom.

MEDITERRANEAN SEA
Nile Delta
Alexandria
Giza • Memphis
Saqqara
El-Amarna

LOWER EGYPT   Valley of the Kings — Karnak
Thebes   Luxor
• Aswan

• Abu Simbel

RED SEA

UPPER EGYPT

River Nile

NUBIAN DESERT

▲ Egypt was split into Lower Egypt (Nile Delta) and Upper Egypt (Nile Valley). Desert conditions meant that people settled along the banks of the Nile.

▼ Historians have divided Egyptian history into a number of periods depending on who was ruling Egypt at the time.

King Narmer, also called Menes, unites Egypt and records his deeds on the Narmer palette

Egypt's first pyramid, the Step Pyramid, was built in 2650 BC

People introduced gods for all different areas of life

The Hyksos people invaded in 1670 BC and introduced the chariot

Nilometers kept track of the height of the river, which was important for crops

3100–2750 BC
EARLY DYNASTIC PERIOD
(Dynasties I and II)

2750–2250 BC
OLD KINGDOM
(Dynasties III–VI)

2250–2025 BC
FIRST INTERMEDIATE PERIOD
(Dynasties VII–X)

2025–1627 BC
MIDDLE KINGDOM
(Dynasties XI–XIII)

1648–1539 BC
SECOND INTERMEDIATE PERIOD
(Dynasties XIV–XVII)

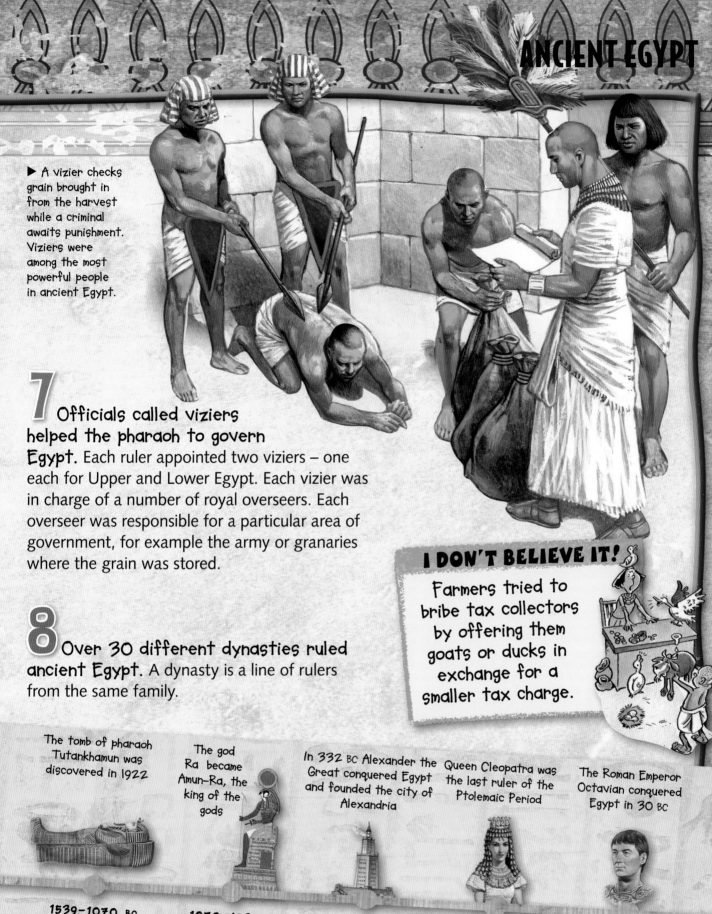

▶ A vizier checks grain brought in from the harvest while a criminal awaits punishment. Viziers were among the most powerful people in ancient Egypt.

7 Officials called viziers helped the pharaoh to govern Egypt. Each ruler appointed two viziers – one each for Upper and Lower Egypt. Each vizier was in charge of a number of royal overseers. Each overseer was responsible for a particular area of government, for example the army or granaries where the grain was stored.

8 Over 30 different dynasties ruled ancient Egypt. A dynasty is a line of rulers from the same family.

I DON'T BELIEVE IT!

Farmers tried to bribe tax collectors by offering them goats or ducks in exchange for a smaller tax charge.

The tomb of pharaoh Tutankhamun was discovered in 1922

The god Ra became Amun-Ra, the king of the gods

In 332 BC Alexander the Great conquered Egypt and founded the city of Alexandria

Queen Cleopatra was the last ruler of the Ptolemaic Period

The Roman Emperor Octavian conquered Egypt in 30 BC

1539–1070 BC
NEW KINGDOM
(Dynasties
XVIII–XX)

1070–653 BC
THIRD
INTERMEDIATE PERIOD
(Dynasties XXI–XXV)

664–332 BC
LATE PERIOD
(Dynasties
XXVI–XXXI)

332–30 BC
PTOLEMAIC PERIOD

30 BC–AD 395
ROMAN PERIOD

Magnificent monuments

9 The pyramids at Giza are more than 4500 years old. They were built for three kings, Khufu, Khafre and Menkaure. The biggest, the Great Pyramid, took more than 20 years to build. Thousands of workers were needed to complete the job.

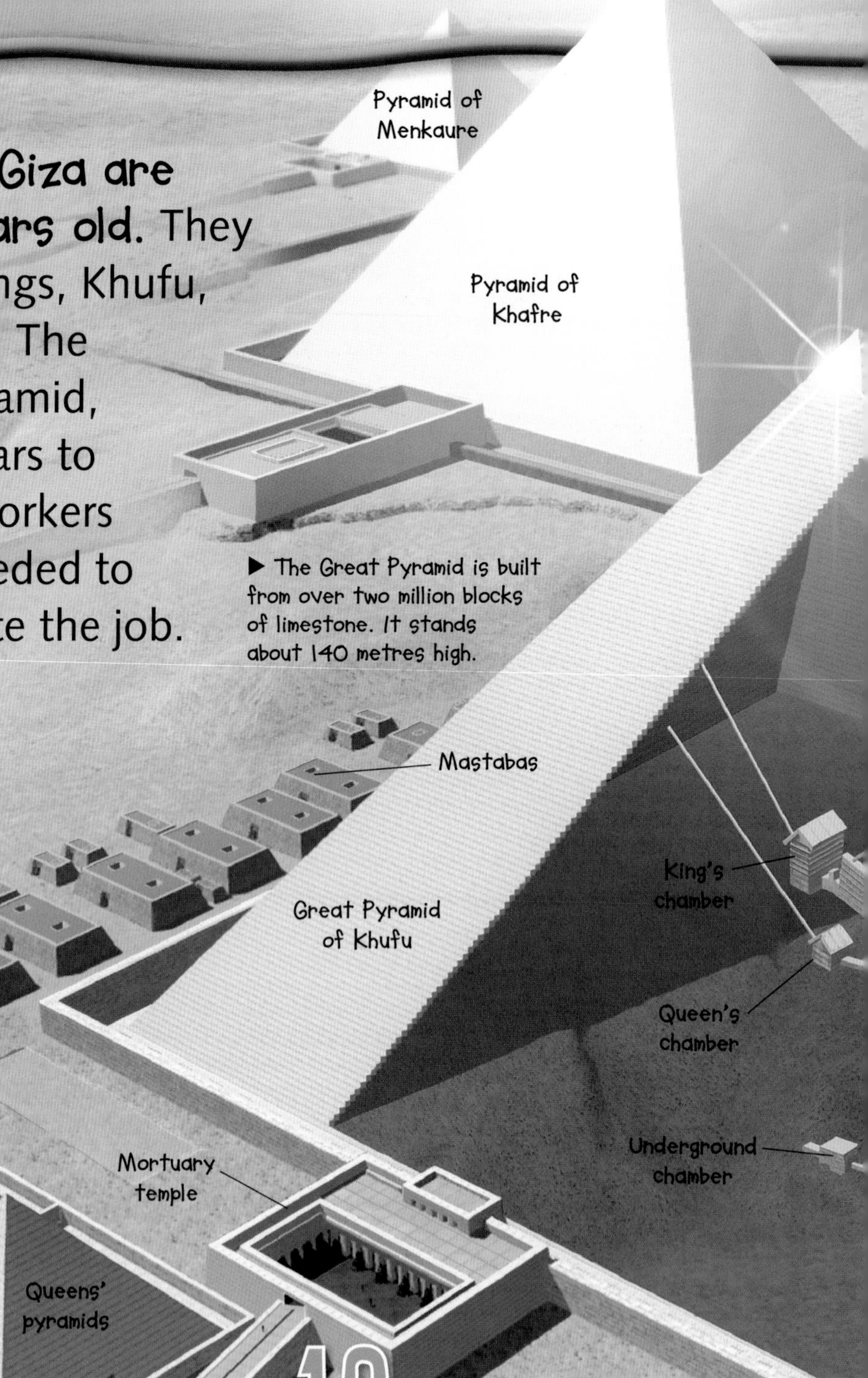

Pyramid of Menkaure
Pyramid of Khafre
Mastabas
King's chamber
Great Pyramid of Khufu
Queen's chamber
Underground chamber
Mortuary temple
Queens' pyramids

▶ The Great Pyramid is built from over two million blocks of limestone. It stands about 140 metres high.

10 The Great Pyramid, the biggest of the three pyramids, was built as a burial place for King Khufu. He ordered three smaller pyramids to be built beside it – for his three main wives. The boat that probably carried Khufu's body to his tomb was buried in a pit alongside the pyramid.

QUIZ

1. For which king was the Great Pyramid built?
2. In the Great Pyramid, which corridor lead to the king's chamber?
3. Where was the first step pyramid built?

Answers:
1. King Khufu 2. The Grand Gallery 3. Saqqara

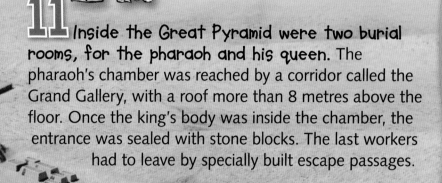

11 Inside the Great Pyramid were two burial rooms, for the pharaoh and his queen. The pharaoh's chamber was reached by a corridor called the Grand Gallery, with a roof more than 8 metres above the floor. Once the king's body was inside the chamber, the entrance was sealed with stone blocks. The last workers had to leave by specially built escape passages.

Western cemetery

Grand Gallery

Entrance

12 The Great Sphinx at Giza guards the way to Khafre's pyramid. It is a huge stone statue with the body of a lion and the head of a human.

▶ The features on the face of the Great Sphinx were carved to look like those of pharaoh Khafre.

13 Tomb robbers broke into the pyramids to steal the fabulous treasures inside. To make things difficult for the robbers, pyramid builders added heavy doors of granite and built false corridors.

14 The earliest pyramids had stepped sides. The steps were like a giant staircase, which the pharaoh could climb to reach the gods. The first step pyramid was built in the desert at Saqqara in about 2650 BC.

Supreme beings

15 The ancient Egyptians worshipped many gods and goddesses. The most important was Ra, the sun god. People believed that he was swallowed up each evening by the sky goddess Nut. During the night Ra travelled the underworld and was reborn each morning.

16 A god was often shown as an animal, or as half-human, half-animal. Bastet was goddess of cats, musicians and dancers. Cats were sacred in ancient Egypt. When a pet cat died, it was wrapped and laid in a cat-shaped coffin before burial in a cat cemetery. The moon god Thoth usually had the head of an ibis, but he was sometimes shown as a baboon. People believed that hieroglyphic writing came from Thoth.

Amun-Ra
Sun god

▶ Crocodiles were kept at the temples of the god Sobek.

Nut
Sky goddess

Sobek
God of the Nile

Bastet
Goddess of cats and music

◀ The sun god Ra was popular in Lower Egypt. The people of Upper Egypt linked him to their own god Amun, so both gods became known as Amun-Ra.

17

As god of the dead, Osiris was in charge of the underworld. Ancient Egyptians believed that dead people travelled to the kingdom of the underworld below the Earth. Osiris and his wife Isis were the parents of the god Horus, protector of the pharaoh.

18

Anubis was in charge of preparing bodies to be mummified. This work was known as embalming. Because jackals were often found near cemeteries, Anubis, who watched over the dead, was given the form of a jackal. Egyptian priests often wore Anubis masks.

19

Pharaoh Amenhotep IV worshipped one god — Aten the creator. He closed down temples to all other gods and even changed his name to Akhenaten, which means 'Spirit of Aten'.

Thoth
Moon god

Osiris
God of the dead

Horus
God of the sky

Isis
Goddess of rebirth

Anubis
God of the underworld

In tombs and temples

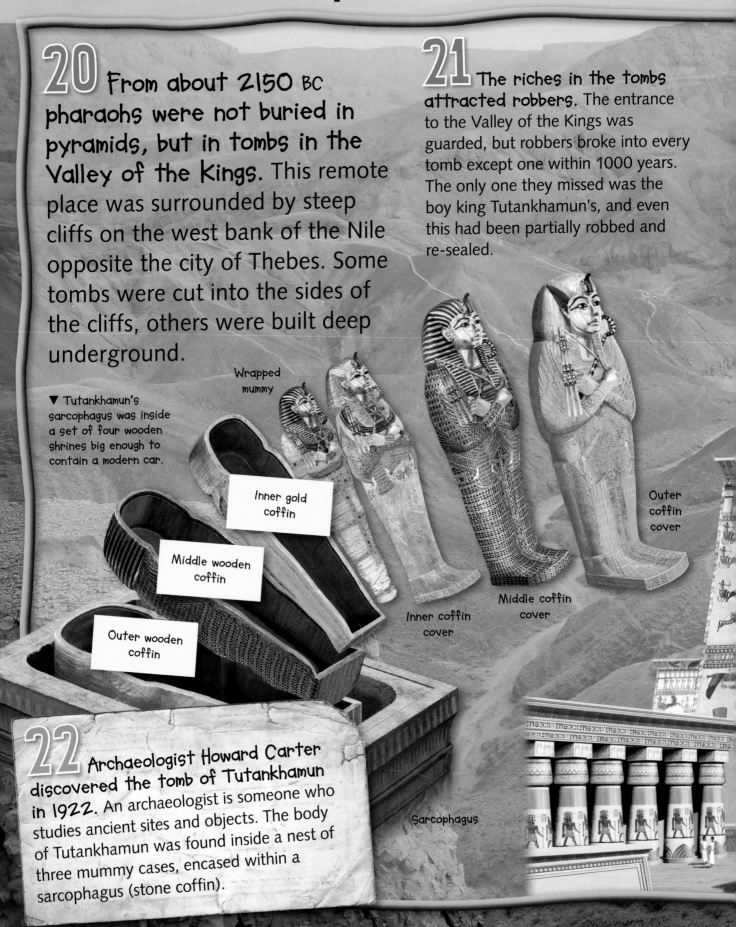

20 From about 2150 BC pharaohs were not buried in pyramids, but in tombs in the Valley of the Kings. This remote place was surrounded by steep cliffs on the west bank of the Nile opposite the city of Thebes. Some tombs were cut into the sides of the cliffs, others were built deep underground.

21 The riches in the tombs attracted robbers. The entrance to the Valley of the Kings was guarded, but robbers broke into every tomb except one within 1000 years. The only one they missed was the boy king Tutankhamun's, and even this had been partially robbed and re-sealed.

▼ Tutankhamun's sarcophagus was inside a set of four wooden shrines big enough to contain a modern car.

Wrapped mummy

Inner gold coffin

Middle wooden coffin

Outer wooden coffin

Inner coffin cover

Middle coffin cover

Outer coffin cover

22 Archaeologist Howard Carter discovered the tomb of Tutankhamun in 1922. An archaeologist is someone who studies ancient sites and objects. The body of Tutankhamun was found inside a nest of three mummy cases, encased within a sarcophagus (stone coffin).

Sarcophagus

23 The Egyptians built fabulous temples to worship their gods. Powerful priests ruled over the temples, and the riches and lands attached to them. Many of the finest temples were dedicated to Amun-Ra, king of the gods.

24 Temples were sacred places. Before being allowed to enter, temple visitors had to shave off their hair and eyebrows.

25 Building work at the Temples of Karnak lasted 1700 years from about 1900 BC. There were three great temples dedicated to the gods Amun-Re, Mut and Montu plus dozens of smaller temples and chapels. Today, millions of people flock to the area to see the remains of the once splendid temple structures.

▼ The courtyard in the Temple of Amun-Re at Karnak was entered through a massive gateway, or pylon, about 17 metres tall.

Big building blocks

26 Each block used to build the Great Pyramid weighed as much as two and a half adult elephants! Labourers used copper chisels and saws to cut and shape the stones before dragging them on wooden sledges to the base of the pyramid.

▶ Pyramids were built using large blocks of stone dragged into position by teams of workmen.

The finished pyramids had a bright, white casing of polished limestone to reflect the rays of the Sun, and the top may have been covered by gold leaf

The huge stones had to be levered into exactly the right position

Wooden sledge for dragging stone blocks

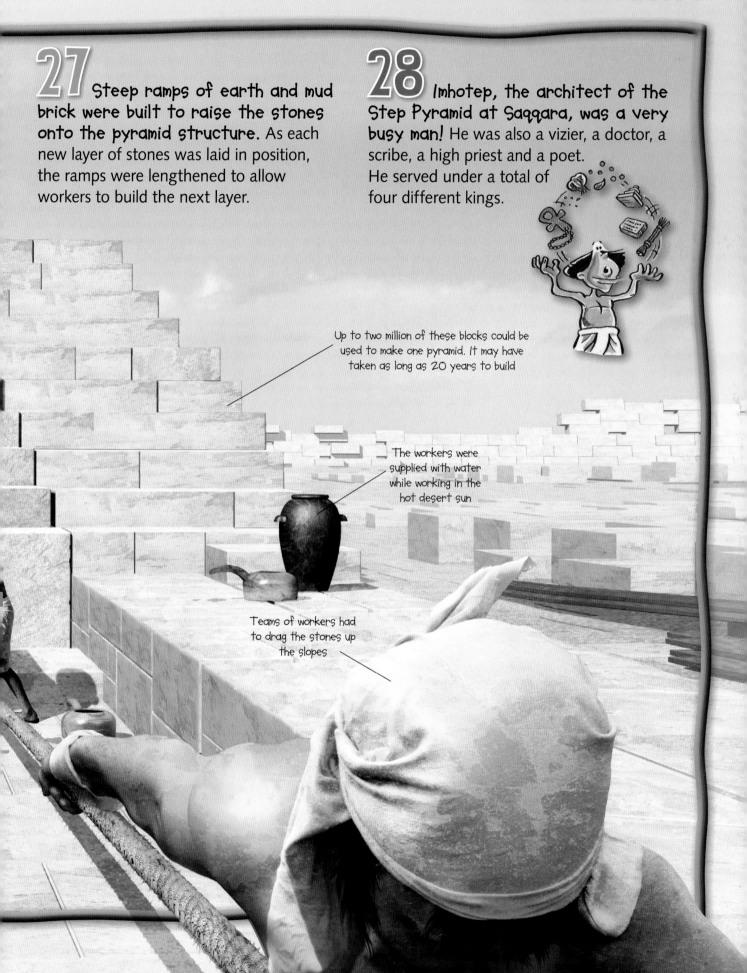

27 Steep ramps of earth and mud brick were built to raise the stones onto the pyramid structure. As each new layer of stones was laid in position, the ramps were lengthened to allow workers to build the next layer.

28 Imhotep, the architect of the Step Pyramid at Saqqara, was a very busy man! He was also a vizier, a doctor, a scribe, a high priest and a poet. He served under a total of four different kings.

Up to two million of these blocks could be used to make one pyramid. It may have taken as long as 20 years to build

The workers were supplied with water while working in the hot desert sun

Teams of workers had to drag the stones up the slopes

Making mummies

29 Making a mummy was skilled work. First the brain, stomach, lungs and other organs were removed, but the heart was left in place. Next, the body was covered with salts and left to dry for up to 40 days. The dried body was washed and filled with linen and other stuffing to keep its shape. Then it was oiled and wrapped in linen bandages.

31 Animals were made into mummies too. A nobleman might be buried with a mummy of his pet cat. Mummification was expensive, so people only preserved animals in this way to offer them to the gods. One mummified crocodile discovered by archaeologists was over 4.5 metres long.

Priest wearing Anubis mask reads prayers

Canopic jars used to store organs

Amulets (charms) placed inside bandages

30 Body parts were removed from the dead person and stored in special containers. The stomach, intestines, lungs and liver were cut out and stored in four separate containers called canopic jars.

32 **A mask was fitted over the face of a mummy.** The ancient Egyptians believed that the mask would help the dead person's spirit to recognize the mummy later on. A pharaoh's mummy mask was made of gold and precious stones.

▼ The process of making mummies took place in sacred workshops and was accompanied by rituals and prayers.

33 **When ready for burial, a mummy was placed inside a special case.** Some cases were simple wooden boxes, but others were shaped like mummies and richly decorated. The mummy case of an important person, such as a pharaoh or a nobleman, was sealed inside a stone coffin called a sarcophagus.

It took many years of training to become a mummy-maker

Hundreds of metres of bandages were used

War and enemies

34 Foot soldiers carried metal swords and spears, with shields made of wood or ox hide. Later, soldiers were protected by body armour made from strips of leather.

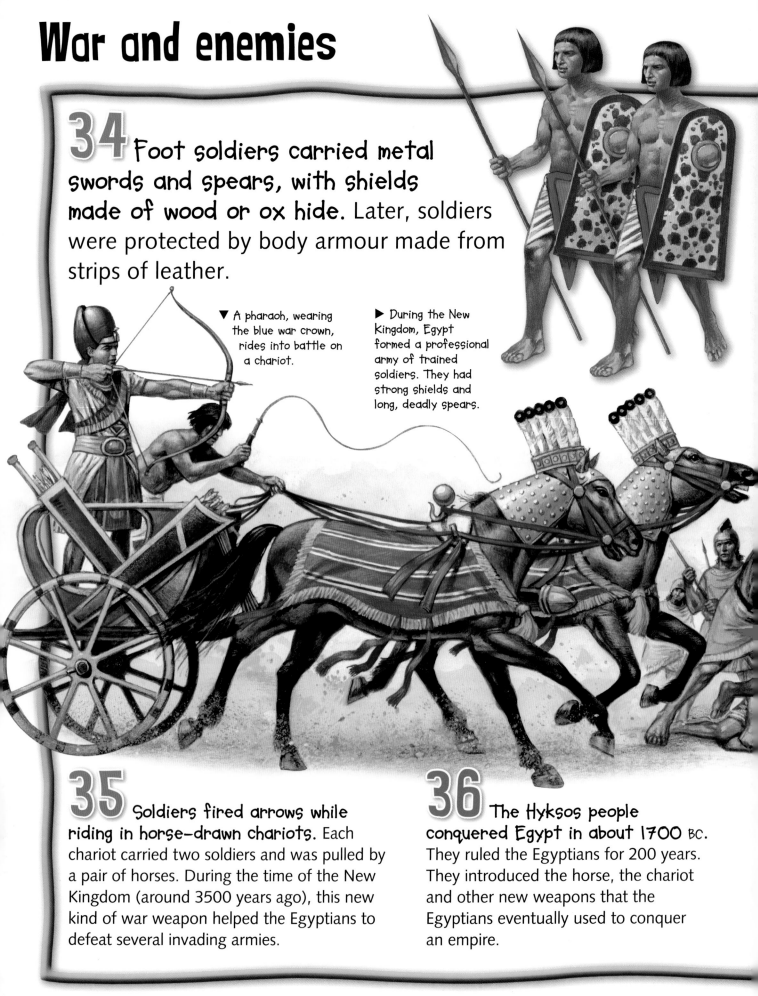

▼ A pharaoh, wearing the blue war crown, rides into battle on a chariot.

▶ During the New Kingdom, Egypt formed a professional army of trained soldiers. They had strong shields and long, deadly spears.

35 Soldiers fired arrows while riding in horse-drawn chariots. Each chariot carried two soldiers and was pulled by a pair of horses. During the time of the New Kingdom (around 3500 years ago), this new kind of war weapon helped the Egyptians to defeat several invading armies.

36 The Hyksos people conquered Egypt in about 1700 BC. They ruled the Egyptians for 200 years. They introduced the horse, the chariot and other new weapons that the Egyptians eventually used to conquer an empire.

37 A Macedonian general called Ptolemy won control of Egypt in 323 BC. He was the first of several rulers who made up the Ptolemaic dynasty. Under the Ptolemies, the city of Alexandria, on the Mediterranean Sea, became the new Egyptian capital and an important city for art and culture.

I DON'T BELIEVE IT!

Soldiers who fought bravely in battle were awarded golden fly medals – for 'buzzing' the enemy so successfully!

38 The Sea People attacked Egypt during the reign of Rameses III. These raiders came from the northeastern corner of the Mediterranean. Rameses sent a fleet of ships to defeat them.

◀ The great harbours at Alexandria were guarded by the huge Pharos, the first lighthouse in the world and one of the Seven Wonders of the Ancient World.

Bartering and buying

39 Before 500 BC, Egyptian traders did not use money to buy and sell goods. Instead they bartered (exchanged goods) with other traders. Merchants visited lands bordering the Mediterranean Sea as well as lands to the south. They offered goods such as gold, a paper called papyrus, and cattle.

41 Egyptians traded with a large number of countries in the Middle East and Africa. Traders brought back silver from Syria, cedar wood, oils and horses from Lebanon, copper from Cyprus, a gem called lapis lazuli from Afghanistan, and ebony wood and ivory from central Africa.

40 People met at market places to exchange goods. Items such as food or textiles could be swapped for exotic goods. Fly swatters made from giraffe tails were a popular fashion item in ancient Egypt.

42 Merchants brought back exotic goods from the land of Nubia, to the south of Egypt. These included leopard skins, elephant tusks, ostrich feathers — and slaves. One of the main trading posts where goods were exchanged was the town of Kerma, on the river Nile beyond Egypt.

▶ A painting shows men from Nubia bringing goods to Egypt.

▲ A busy Egyptian trading market with people bartering for goods.

43 When goods were sold they were weighed using a balance and special copper weights called deben. An item could be exchanged for its equivalent weight in copper. A bed, for example, had a value of 25 deben. Pieces of gold and silver were also weighed and used as payment.

The farmer's year

44 The farming year was divided into three seasons: the flood, the growing period and the harvest. Most people worked on the land, but farmers could not work between July and November because the land was flooded. Instead, they helped to build the pyramids and royal palaces.

▲ Water is lifted onto a field using a shaduf, just as is done in Egypt today.

45 The river Nile used to flood its banks in July each year. The flood waters left a strip of rich, black soil, about 10 kilometres wide, along each bank. Apart from these fertile strips and a few scattered oases (pools of water in the desert) the rest of the land was mainly just sand.

47 Water was lifted from the Nile using a shaduf. It was a long pole with a wooden bucket hanging from a rope at one end, and a weight at the other. The pole was supported by a wooden frame. One person working alone could operate a shaduf.

◀ Tax collectors would often decide how rich a person was by counting how many cattle he owned.

46 Egyptian farmers had to water their crops because of the hot, dry climate with no rain. They dug special channels around their fields along which the waters of the Nile could flow. In this way farmers could water their crops all year round. This was called irrigation.

▲ Almost no rain fell on the dry, dusty farmland of ancient Egypt. No crops could grow properly without the water from the Nile.

48 Wooden ploughs pulled by oxen prepared the soil for planting. Seeds were mainly planted by hand. At harvest time, wooden sickles edged with stone teeth were used to cut the crops.

▲ A man ploughs a field of wheat or barley, assisted by his wife.

49 Harvesting grain was only the start of the process. In the threshing room people would beat the grain to separate it from the chaff, the shell, of the grain. It was then winnowed. Men would throw the grain and chaff into the air and fan away the chaff. The heavier grain dropped straight to the floor. The grain was then gathered up and taken to the granary to be stored.

50 Wheat and barley (for bread and beer) were the two main crops grown by the ancient Egyptians. They also grew grapes (for wine) and flax (to make linen). A huge variety of fruits and vegetables grew in the fertile soil, including dates, figs, cucumbers, melons, onions, peas, leeks and lettuces.

51 Instead of using scarecrows, Egyptian farmers hired young boys. They had to have a loud voice and a good aim with a slingshot to scare the birds away from the crops.

▼ Winnowers separate the grain from the chaff.

52 Egyptian farmers kept cattle as well as goats, sheep, ducks and geese. Some farmers kept bees to produce honey, which was used for sweetening cakes and other foods.

Getting around

53 The main method of transporting goods in ancient Egypt was by boat along the Nile. The Nile is the world's longest river. It flows across the entire length of the desert lands of Egypt.

54 The earliest kinds of boat were made from papyrus reeds. They were propelled by a long pole and, later on, by oars. Gradually, wooden boats replaced the reed ones, and sails were added.

▲ Early boats were made from bundles of reeds tied together.

55 A magnificent carved boat was built to carry the body of King Khufu at his funeral. More than 43 metres long, it was built from planks of cedar wood. The boat was buried in a special pit next to the Great Pyramid.

▲ The Nile results from the joining of three great rivers – the White Nile, the Blue Nile and the Atbara.

56 Transporting cattle across the Nile could be difficult. Wide-bodied cargo boats were used to ferry cattle across the Nile. The animals stood on the deck during the crossing.

◄ In 1954, King Khufu's funerary boat was found buried at the foot of the Great Pyramid.

57 Wooden barges carried blocks of limestone across the river Nile for the pyramids and temples. The stone came from quarries on the opposite bank to the site of the pyramids. The granite used to build the insides of the pyramids came from much farther away – from quarries at Aswan 800 kilometres upstream.

▼ A merchant river boat powered by sails or oars.

▲ Blocks of stone are loaded on a boat to be taken along the Nile to a building site.

Who's who?

58 **People were divided into classes.** Farmers and tradesmen worked in businesses owned by the state or temples, and could not move class. Scribes and merchants could move, but were barely richer than farmers and tradesmen. Nobles and priests organized Egypt under the pharaoh's rule.

◄ The arrangement of Egyptian society can be shown as a pyramid shape. The pharaoh sits at the top, with unskilled labourers at the bottom.

Viziers and priests

Scribes and noblemen

Craftworkers and dancers

Peasant workers

59 **The man was the head of the household.** On his father's death, the eldest son inherited the family's land and riches. Women had rights and privileges too. They could own property and carry out business deals, and women from wealthy families could become doctors or priestesses.

60 **Most ancient Egyptians lived along the banks of the river Nile or in the river valley.** As Egypt became more powerful they spread out, up along the river Nile and around the Mediterranean Sea. Others lived by oases, pools of water in the desert.

► Family life played an important role in ancient Egypt. Couples could adopt children if they were unable to have their own.

61 Rich families had several servants, who worked as maids, cooks and gardeners. In large houses the servants had their own quarters separate from those of the family.

62 Wealthy Egyptians wanted servants in the afterlife too. They were buried with models of servants, called shabtis, that were meant to come to life and look after their dead owner!

63 Dogs and cats were the main pets. Egyptians also kept pet monkeys and sometimes flocks of tame doves. Some people trained their pet baboons to climb fig trees and pick the ripe fruits.

64 Young children played with wooden and clay toys. Popular toys were carved animals – often with moving parts – spinning tops, toy horses, dolls and clay balls. Children also played games that are still played today, such as leapfrog and tug-o'-war.

Home sweet home

65 Houses were made from mud bricks dried in the sun. Straw and pebbles were added to the mud to make it strong. Tree trunks supported the flat roofs. Inside walls were plastered and often painted. The rich lived in big houses with several storeys. The poor often lived in a single room.

66 Rich families lived in spacious villas in the countryside. A typical villa had a pond filled with fish, a walled garden and an orchard of fruit trees.

67 Homes were furnished with wooden chairs, tables, chests and carved beds. A three- or four-legged footstool was a common item of furniture. Reed mats covered the floors.

Pots and plates were made of clay and fired in a hot kiln.

Bricks were made of mud and clay strengthened with straw and pebbles. They were packed in wooden frames and left to harden in the sun.

68 Food was cooked in a clay oven or over an open fire. Most kitchens had a cylinder-shaped oven made from bricks of baked clay. Wood or charcoal was burnt as fuel, and food was placed in two-handled pottery saucepans to cook.

69 Pottery lamps provided lighting. The container was filled with oil and a wick made of cotton or flax was burned. Houses had very small windows, and sometimes none at all, so there was often little natural light. Small windows kept out the strong sunlight, helping to keep houses cool.

Bread was the staple food. It was baked in a hot oven. The poor ate coarse brown bread and the rich ate white.

Beer was stored in pottery jars. Spices and dates were added to improve the taste.

Clothes were made with linen woven on a loom, from the fibres of the flax plant.

70 In most Egyptian homes there was a small shrine. Here, members of the family worshipped their household god.

71 In Egypt it was good to eat with your fingers! In rich households, servants would even bring jugs of water between courses so that people could rinse their hands.

Dressing up

72 Egyptians wore lucky charms called amulets. The charms were meant to protect the wearer from evil spirits and to bring good luck. One of the most popular ones was the eye of the god Horus. Children wore amulets shaped like fish to protect them from drowning in the river Nile.

▲ Scarab amulets were worn for good fortune. They were carved from gems and semi-precious stones.

73 Both men and women wore eye make-up. A black eye make-up, called kohl, was made from ground-up raw metals mixed with oil. The Egyptians believed it had healing powers and could restore bad eyesight and fight infections. People also used rouge for the cheeks and lips, face powder, paint for fingernails and hair dyes.

◄ A wealthy woman applying eye make-up before putting on her wig.

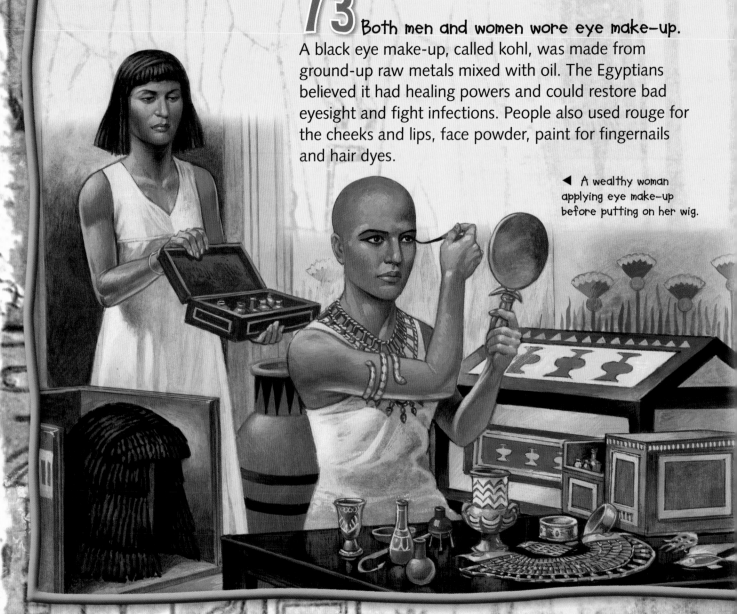

74 **Most clothes were made from light-coloured linen.** Women wore long dresses, often with pleated cloaks. Noblewomen's dresses were made of the best cloth with beads sewn onto it. Noblemen wore either robes or kilt-like skirts, a piece of linen wrapped around the waist and tied in a decorative knot.

▶ Wealthy Egyptians wore long robes of pleated linen.

MAKE A MAGIC EYE CHARM

You will need:
self-hardening modelling clay
length of leather strip or thick cord
pencil   poster paints
paintbrush   varnish

1. Knead the clay until soft and then shape into the charm.

2. Add extra clay for the pupil of the eye and at the top of the charm. Use the pencil to make the top piece into a loop.

3. Leave the clay to harden. Paint in bright colours and leave to dry.

4. Varnish, then thread the leather strip or cord through the loop and wear your charm for extra luck.

75 **Sandals were made from papyrus and other reeds.** Kings and queens, rich people and courtiers wore padded leather ones. Footwear was a luxury item, and most ordinary people walked around barefoot. Colourful pictures of sandals were even painted onto the feet of mummies!

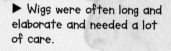

▶ Wigs were often long and elaborate and needed a lot of care.

▼ Egyptians cared for their wigs with combs made of wood and ivory. They used ivory pins to keep their hair in place.

Ivory comb

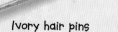
Ivory hair pins

Wooden comb

76 **Wealthy people wore wigs made from human hair or sheep's wool.** Wigs were kept on a stand when not being worn. Girls wore their hair in pigtails, while boys mostly had shaved heads, sometimes with a plaited lock on one side.

35

Baking and brewing

77 **Bread was the most important food.** Harvested grain was stored in granaries until needed. Beer was the most popular drink. It was very thick and had to be strained before drinking. Models of brewers were left in tombs to ensure the dead person had plenty of beer in the next world!

▼ Beer was made from grain and water. Egyptian beer did not keep well and needed to be drunk within a day or two.

Workers treading on grain and water mixture

Water and grain fermenting in jars

The fermented brew is sieved to remove pieces of grain

Water is poured into a jar of grain to be mixed

BANQUET MENU

A huge choice of food was served at banquets for wealthy Egyptians. Meats such as duck, goose, gazelle and heron, fresh fruits and vegetables, sweet pastries and cakes, with lots of beer and grape or date wine to drink. Choose the food for a banquet and design a decorative menu for your guests.

78 A rough kind of bread was baked from wheat or barley. It often contained gritty pieces that wore down people's teeth. Historians have discovered this by studying the teeth of mummies.

Bread dough is kneaded to make the mix supple and nutritious

An overseer ensured the quality of the finished product

Grain could be made into flour by pounding or by grinding

▲ Bread was made from grain that had been ground into flour and mixed with water. It could be stored for a few days before being eaten.

Hard day's work

79 Scribes were very important people. These highly skilled men kept records of everything that happened from day to day. They recorded the materials used for building work, the number of cattle, and the crops that had been gathered for the royal family, the government and the temples.

80 Libraries in ancient Egypt held thousands of papyrus scrolls. They covered subjects such as law, astronomy, medicine and geography. Most Egyptians could not read or write, so libraries were used by educated people such as scribes and doctors.

81 Imagine if there were 700 letters in the alphabet! That was how many hieroglyphs Egyptian school children had to learn. Hieroglyphs were symbols that the Egyptians used for writing. Some symbols stood for words and some for sounds. Only boys went to schools for scribes, where they first learned how to read and write hieroglyphs.

▼ Only the sons of scribes could undergo the strict scribe training, which began as early as the age of nine.

Pupils sat cross-legged on the floor and raised their hands to answer a question

Boys wore a ponytail known as the 'side-lock of youth'

82 Most people worked as craftworkers or farm labourers. Craftworkers included carpenters, potters, weavers, jewellers, shoemakers, glassblowers and perfume makers. Many sold their goods from small shops in the towns. They were kept busy making items for the pharaoh and wealthy people.

▶ Craftworkers produced statues and furniture for the pharaoh. Workers such as these often had their own areas within a town. The village of Deir el-Medina was built specially for those who worked on tombs in the Valley of the Kings.

83 A typical lunch for a worker consisted of bread and onions. They may also have had a cucumber, washed down with a drink of beer.

85 Slaves were often prisoners who were captured from enemies. They also came from the countries of Kush and Nubia. Life as a slave was not all bad. A slave could own land and buy goods – and even buy his freedom.

84 The base of the Great Pyramid takes up almost as much space as five football pitches! Huge quantities of stone were needed to build these monuments. The Egyptians quarried limestone, sandstone and granite for their buildings. In the surrounding desert they mined gold for decorations.

QUIZ

1. Were girls sent to scribe school?
2. Where did Egyptians get their slaves?
3. Who used libraries?
4. Where was gold found?

Answers:
1. No, only boys 2. From Kush and Nubia 3. Scribes and doctors 4. In the deserts of Egypt

Clever Egyptians

86 The insides of many Egyptian tombs were decorated with brightly coloured wall paintings. The scenes showed what the Egyptians hoped life in the next world would be like.

▲ The Egyptians believed that these wall paintings would come to life in the next world.

87 Sculptors carved enormous statues of their pharaohs and gods. Stone statues up to 20 metres tall were placed outside tombs or temples to guard the entrance. Inside a tomb was a small wooden statue of the dead person where the ka, or life force, of the person could rest. Inside temples the holiest statue of a god would be made of silver, ivory or gold.

▲ Huge stone statues guard the entrance to the temple of Abu Simbel. When the temple was rediscovered in 1817, it was almost covered by sand.

88 There were three different calendars. A 365-day farming calendar was made up of three seasons of four months. An astronomical calendar was based on observations of the star Sirius, which reappeared at the start of the flood season. Priests kept a calendar based on the movements of the Moon, which told them when to perform ceremonies for the moon god.

89 Astronomers recorded what they saw in the night skies. The Egyptian calendar was based on the movement of Sirius, the brightest star in the sky. The Egyptians used their knowledge of astronomy to build temples that lined up with certain stars.

90 Nilometers were used to study the annual river floods. As the water rose it entered a chamber marked with lines to measure the height of the flood and where priests could see how much mud the flood was bringing.

▶ A doctor consults a papyrus roll while treating a patient.

91 Egyptian doctors knew how to set broken bones and treat illnesses such as fevers. They used medicines made from plants such as garlic and juniper to treat sick people. The Egyptians had a good knowledge of the basic workings of the human body.

From pictures to words

92 **The Egyptians had no paper – they wrote on papyrus.** It was made from papyrus reeds that grew on the banks of the Nile. At first papyrus was sold as long strips, or scrolls, tied with string. Later, papyrus sheets were put into books. Papyrus lasts a long time – sheets have survived 3000 years to the present day.

93 **Ink was made by mixing water with soot, charcoal or coloured minerals.** Scribes wrote in ink on papyrus scrolls, using reed brushes with specially shaped ends.

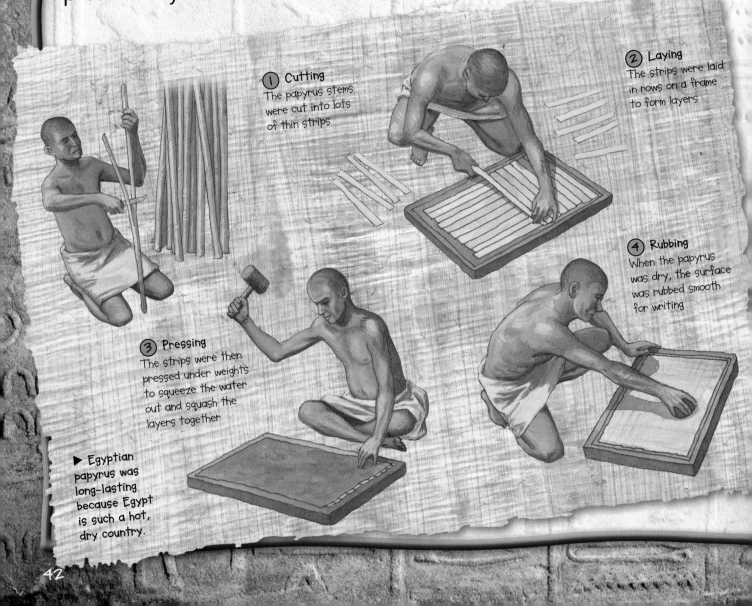

① **Cutting**
The papyrus stems were cut into lots of thin strips

② **Laying**
The strips were laid in rows on a frame to form layers

④ **Rubbing**
When the papyrus was dry, the surface was rubbed smooth for writing

③ **Pressing**
The strips were then pressed under weights to squeeze the water out and squash the layers together

▶ Egyptian papyrus was long-lasting because Egypt is such a hot, dry country.

94

The Rosetta Stone was found in 1799 by a French soldier in Egypt. It is a large stone onto which three kinds of writing have been carved: hieroglyphics, demotics (a simpler form of hieroglyphics), and Greek. All three sets of writing give an account of the coronation of King Ptolemy V.

▲ The Rosetta Stone in the British Museum. The stone itself is made of granite, and is a broken part of a bigger slab.

95

In the 5th century BC a Greek historian called Herodotus wrote about life in ancient Egypt. As he travelled across the country he observed and wrote about people's daily lives, and their religion and customs such as embalming and mummification.

▼ The name of Rameses II written inside a cartouche to show he was a pharaoh.

96

The hieroglyphs of a ruler's name were written inside an oval-shaped frame called a cartouche. The pharaoh's cartouche was carved on pillars and temple walls, painted on tomb walls and mummy cases, and written on official documents.

97

The Egyptians used a system of picture writing called hieroglyphics. Each hieroglyph represented an object or a sound. For example, the picture of a lion represented the sound 'l' and a basket represented the word 'lord'. Scribes wrote hieroglyphs on papyrus scrolls or carved them into stone.

PICTURE-WRITING

Below is a hieroglyphic alphabet. The name 'Jane' has been written in hieroglyphs. Can you write your name?

43

Heroes and heroines

98 Rameses II built more temples than any other Egyptian ruler. Two of his greatest achievements are the huge rock-cut temple at Abu Simbel and the Great Hall at Karnak. He also finished building the mortuary temple of Seti I at Luxor. After his death a further nine pharaohs were given the name Rameses.

99 Queen Hatshepsut was often depicted wearing men's clothing and a false beard. She was the wife of Thutmose II. On his death Hatshepsut took the title of pharaoh and adopted the royal symbols of the double crown, the crook, the flail (whip) – and also the ceremonial beard!

100 Queen Cleopatra VII was the last ruler of an independent ancient Egypt. She fell in love with Julius Caesar, a Roman emperor, and later married a Roman general, Mark Antony. In 30 BC, Cleopatra killed herself with a poisonous snake when the Romans conquered Egypt.

▲ The temple of Abu Simbel is now a famous tourist attraction and a UNESCO World Heritage Site. More than 150,000 people visit every year.

101 Tutankhamun is probably the most famous pharaoh of all. His tomb, with its fabulous treasure of over 5000 objects, was discovered complete in 1922. Tutankhamun was only nine years old when he became ruler, and he died at the young age of about 17. He was buried in the Valley of the Kings.

► The head of of Tutankhamun's mummy was covered by a mask made of solid gold, and decorated with jewels.

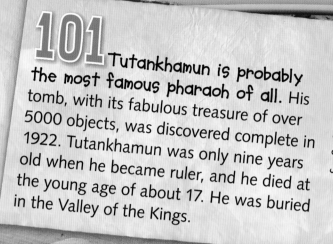

102 King Menes was the first ruler of a united Egypt. He joined together the kingdoms of Upper and Lower Egypt, under one government, in around 3100 BC. Menes was also called Narmer. Archaeologists have found a slate tablet, called the Narmer Palette, that shows him beating his enemies in battle.

103 Thutmose III was a clever general who added new lands to ancient Egypt. Under his leadership, Egypt's armies seized territory in Syria to the north and Palestine to the east. During his reign Thutmose ordered a giant obelisk made of granite to be placed at Heliopolis — it now stands on the bank of the river Thames in London.

ANCIENT GREECE

104 Ancient Greece was a small country, but its people had great ideas. From around 2000 BC, they created a splendid civilization that reached its peak between 500–400 BC. All citizens contributed to a society that respected people's rights, encouraged the best in human nature and lived in harmony with the natural world. Today, we still admire Greek sport, medicine, drama, politics, poetry and art.

▲ The agora (town square) of Athens was a meeting place for citizens and an open-air market. Traders sold fresh fruit and vegetables and craftworkers sold cloth and pottery.

Greek homelands

105 The Greeks thought that they were better than other people. They saw all foreigners as uncivilized 'barbarians' who did not share the same values and beliefs, or follow the Greeks' lifestyle. Even worse, they did not speak or understand the elegant Greek language.

106 Lifestyle was shaped by the seasons. Winters were cold with icy winds, pouring rain and storms. Summers were very hot and dry with droughts, dust and forest fires. Spring was green and fresh – a time to plant crops and fight wars. Autumn with its harvest of ripe olives, grapes and grain was the busiest time for farmers.

▼ Neat rows of olive trees growing on a Greek farm. Olives were mixed with salt then stored in jars to eat, or crushed to make oil.

▼ The Greeks' homeland included mainland Greece and over 2000 islands in the Aegean Sea and the Ionian Sea, together with the coast of Asia Minor.

THRAC

MACEDONIA

Mount Olympus

GREECE

IONIAN SEA

Athens

Olympia

Sparta

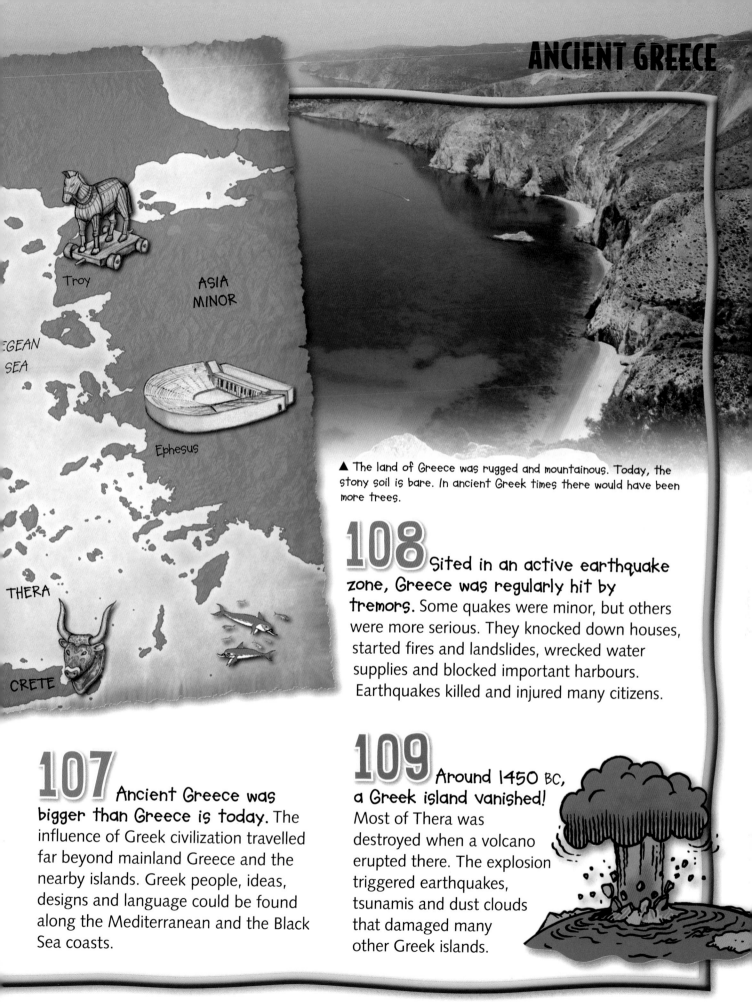

Troy

ASIA MINOR

EGEAN SEA

Ephesus

THERA

CRETE

▲ The land of Greece was rugged and mountainous. Today, the stony soil is bare. In ancient Greek times there would have been more trees.

108 Sited in an active earthquake zone, Greece was regularly hit by tremors. Some quakes were minor, but others were more serious. They knocked down houses, started fires and landslides, wrecked water supplies and blocked important harbours. Earthquakes killed and injured many citizens.

107 Ancient Greece was bigger than Greece is today. The influence of Greek civilization travelled far beyond mainland Greece and the nearby islands. Greek people, ideas, designs and language could be found along the Mediterranean and the Black Sea coasts.

109 Around 1450 BC, a Greek island vanished! Most of Thera was destroyed when a volcano erupted there. The explosion triggered earthquakes, tsunamis and dust clouds that damaged many other Greek islands.

Steeped in history

110 The ancient Greeks were proud of their beautiful country. There were high snowy mountains, swift rushing streams, thick forests, flowery meadows and narrow, fertile plains beside the sea. Around the coast there were thousands of rocky islands, some small and poor, others large and prosperous.

◀ A carved stone figure of a woman found in the Cyclades Islands. The design is very simple but strong and graceful.

▼ This timeline shows some of the important events in the history of ancient Greece.

111 Greek civilization began on the islands. Some of the first evidence of farming in Greece comes from the Cyclades Islands. Around 6000 BC, people living there began to plant grain and build villages. They buried their dead in graves filled with treasures, such as carved marble figures, pottery painted with magic sun symbols and gold and silver jewellery.

TIMELINE OF GREECE

c. 40,000 BC
First people in Greece. They are hunters and gatherers

c. 2000–1450 BC
Minoan civilization on the island of Crete

c. 1250 BC
Traditional date of the Trojan War

c. 900–700 BC
Greek civilization grows strong again

c. 6000 BC
First farmers in Greece

c. 1600–1100 BC
Mycenean civilization on mainland Greece

c. 1100–900 BC
A time of decline – kingdoms weaken, writing stops

c. 776 BC
Traditional date of first Olympic Games

◀ This jar, made around 900 BC, is rather dull and plain. It suggests that times were troubled and Greek people had no money to spare for art.

112 Between 1100–900 BC, the history of Greece is a mystery.
From 2000–1100 BC, powerful kings ruled Greece. They left splendid buildings and objects behind them, and used writing. But between around 1100–900 BC, there were no strong kingdoms, little art, few new buildings – and writing disappeared.

▲ Alexander the Great conquered an empire stretching from Greece to India.

113 Migrants settled in distant lands.
By around 700 BC, Greece was overcrowded. There were too many people, not enough farmland to grow food and some islands were short of water. Greek families left to set up colonies far away, from southern France to North Africa, Turkey and Bulgaria.

114 When the neighbours invaded, Greek power collapsed.
After 431 BC, Greek cities were at war and the fighting weakened them. In 338 BC, Philip II of Macedonia (a kingdom north of Greece) invaded with a large army. After Philip died, his son, Alexander the Great, made Greece part of his mighty empire.

c. 700–500 BC
Greeks set up colonies around Mediterranean Sea

c. 480–479 BC
Greece fights invaders from Persia (now Iran)

c. 338 BC
Philip II of Macedonia conquers Greece

c. 147–146 BC
Romans conquer Greece and Macedonia

c. 500–430 BC
Athens leads Greece, creates amazing art, has democratic government

c. 431–404 BC
Wars between Athens and Sparta

c. 336–323 BC
Alexander the Great of Macedonia and Greece conquers a vast empire

Kings and warriors

115 **King Minos ruled an amazing palace city.** The first great Greek civilization grew up at Knossos on the island of Crete. Historians call it 'Minoan' after its legendary king, Minos. Around 2000 BC, Minoan kings built an amazing palace-city, with rooms for 10,000 people. It was decorated with wonderful frescoes (wall paintings), statues and pottery.

▲ A section of the palace at Knossos on the island of Crete. A succession of powerful kings ruled a rich kingdom here.

116 **Minoan Greeks honoured a monster.** Greek myths describe how a fearsome monster was kept in a labyrinth (underground maze) below the palace. It was called the Minotaur, and it was half-man, half-bull.

▲ Greek legends told how the young hero Theseus bravely entered the labyrinth and killed the Minotaur.

Oule = Hello

Khaire = Goodbye

▶ This golden mask was found in one of the royal tombs at Mycenae. It covered the face of a king who died around 1500 BC.

117 Invaders brought the Greek language. Between around 2100–1700 BC, warriors from the north arrived in mainland Greece. They brought new words with them and their language was copied by everyone else living in Greece.

▼ Works of art found at Knossos include many images of huge, fierce bulls with athletes leaping between their horns in a deadly religious ritual.

118 Mycenae was ruled by warrior kings. Around 1600 BC new kings took control of Minoan lands from forts on the Greek mainland. The greatest fort was at Mycenae, in the far south of Greece. Mycenaean kings sent traders to Egypt and the Near East to exchange Greek pottery and olive oil for gold, tin and amber. They used their wealth to pay for huge tombs in which they were buried.

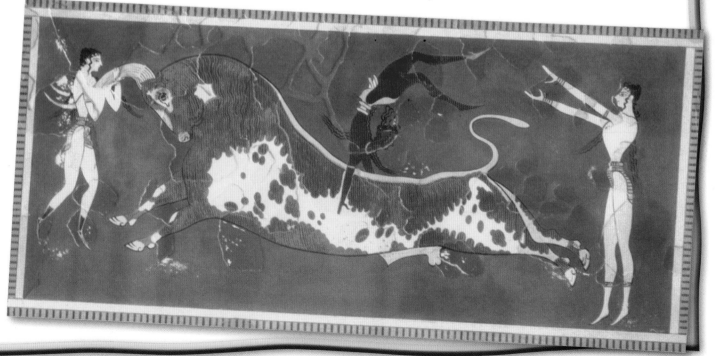

War with Troy

119 A famous Greek poem, the Iliad, describes a terrible war between the Greeks and the Trojans. The Trojans lived in a rich city on the west coast of Asia Minor (now Turkey). The Iliad was first written down around 750 BC. Ancient Greeks said the writer was a blind poet called Homer.

▼ A scene from the 2004 film *Troy*, starring Brad Pitt. The war between the Trojans and the Greeks still thrills people today. Some of the story is legend, but it may be based on real, half-remembered facts.

120 Queen Helen loved a Trojan prince. According to legend, the Trojan War started because Helen, the wife of Greek King Menelaus, ran away with (or was captured by) Paris, a Trojan prince. However, historians believe the main reason for the war was because the Greeks and the Trojans were rival traders.

121 The Greeks could not break through Troy's walls until they thought of a clever plan. They made a huge, hollow, wooden horse, hid warriors inside and persuaded the Trojans to accept it as an offering to the gods. The Trojans hauled the horse into their city, then the Greeks leaped out and defeated them.

122 Odysseus survived to have amazing adventures. Another famous Greek poem tells how the warrior Odysseus fought at Troy, then on the way home survived extraordinary encounters with gods, giants, witches, one-eyed monsters, sea-serpents and a man-eating whirlpool.

▶ The Cyclops was a one-eyed giant. He trapped Odysseus and his soldiers in a cave and planned to eat them. But Odysseus blinded the Cyclops, escaped from the cave and sailed away.

▶ The Iliad describes how, for ten years, the Greeks besieged the city of Troy. They eventually won the war by offering a wooden horse to the Trojans. Once inside the city walls, warriors leapt out of the horse and destroyed the city.

City-states

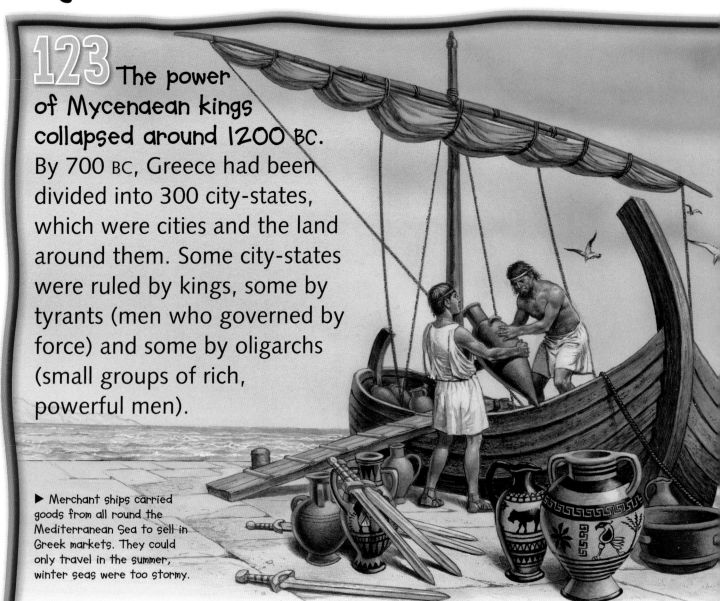

123 The power of Mycenaean kings collapsed around 1200 BC. By 700 BC, Greece had been divided into 300 city-states, which were cities and the land around them. Some city-states were ruled by kings, some by tyrants (men who governed by force) and some by oligarchs (small groups of rich, powerful men).

▶ Merchant ships carried goods from all round the Mediterranean Sea to sell in Greek markets. They could only travel in the summer, winter seas were too stormy.

124 Most city-states grew rich by buying and selling. The agora (market-place) was the centre of many cities. Goods on sale included farm produce such as grain, wine and olive oil, salt from the sea, pottery, woollen blankets, sheepskin cloaks, leather sandals and slaves.

125 Top craftsmen made fine goods for sale. Cities were home to many expert craftsmen. They ran small workshops next to their homes, or worked as slaves in factories owned by rich businessmen. Greek craftworkers were famous for producing fine pottery, stone-carvings, weapons, armour and jewellery.

126 Coins displayed city wealth and pride.
They were invented in the Near East around 600 BC. Their use soon spread to Greece, and each city-state issued its own designs, stamped out of real silver. Coins were often decorated with images of gods and goddesses, heroes, monsters and favourite local animals.

▶ The design on the top coin shows the head of Alexander the Great. The other is decorated with an owl, the symbol of Athens' guardian goddess, Athena.

◀▲ The walls and gates guarding the city of Mycenae were made of huge stone slabs. The gate had a huge sculpture of two lions above it.

127 Cities were defended by strong stone walls.
City-states were proud, independent and quarrelsome. They were often at war with their rivals. They were also in constant danger of attack from neighbouring nations, especially Persia (now Iran). To protect their homes, temples, workshops, market-places and harbours, citizens built strong wooden gates and high stone walls.

▶ Many Greek ships were wrecked together with their cargoes. Some have survived on the seabed for over 2000 years and are studied by divers today.

QUIZ

1. What was a city-state?
2. What was the centre of many cities?
3. What were coins made of?
4. How did the Greeks defend their cities?

Answers:
1. A city and the land around it
2. The agora (market-place) 3. Real silver 4. With strong wooden gates and high stone walls

Citizens, foreigners, slaves

▶ Slaves for sale. Men, women and children captured in war or snatched by pirates were put on display for rich families to buy.

128 Within most city-states, there were different classes of people. Citizens were men who had been born in the city-state, together with their wives and children. Foreigners were traders, sailors or travelling artists and scholars. Slaves belonged to their owners.

129 In wealthy city-states almost half the population were slaves. Household slaves did the shopping, cooking, housework and child care. Gangs of slave-labourers worked for rich citizens or city governments as builders, road-menders, miners and security guards. Slaves could be very badly treated. The conditions for slaves working in mines and on building sites were grim and many died.

130 In 508 BC, Athenian leader Cleisthenes established a new system of government called 'democracy' (rule by the people). All male citizens over 18 years old could speak and vote at city Assemblies, elect the officials that ran their city-state and be elected as city councillors. Women, foreigners, children and slaves had no democratic rights.

131 In Athens, citizens could make speeches at the Assembly to propose new laws for their community. They served as jurors in the city-state law courts, hearing the evidence against accused criminals and deciding whether they were innocent or guilty. Citizens could also take part in debates on important government decisions, such as whether to declare war.

▼ Speeches at the Athenian Assembly were carefully timed (and kept short) so that all citizens would have a chance to share in the debate.

QUIZ
1. What is democracy?
2. Where was it established?
3. What is an ostrakon?
4. What was it used for?

Answers:
1. Rule by the people 2. Athens 3. A piece of broken pottery 4. Voting to ban an unpopular person from Athens. Citizens scratched the person's name on the ostrakon

▼ You can see the names of two unpopular Athenian citizens scratched on these pieces of pottery. Left, top line: Themistokles. Right, top line: Kimon.

132 Once a year, Athenian citizens voted to ban unpopular people from their city for ten years. They scratched the name of the person they wanted to remove on an ostrakon (piece of broken pottery). If 6000 citizens (about a quarter of the whole Assembly) voted to ban the same man, he had to leave the city within ten days.

Mighty Athens

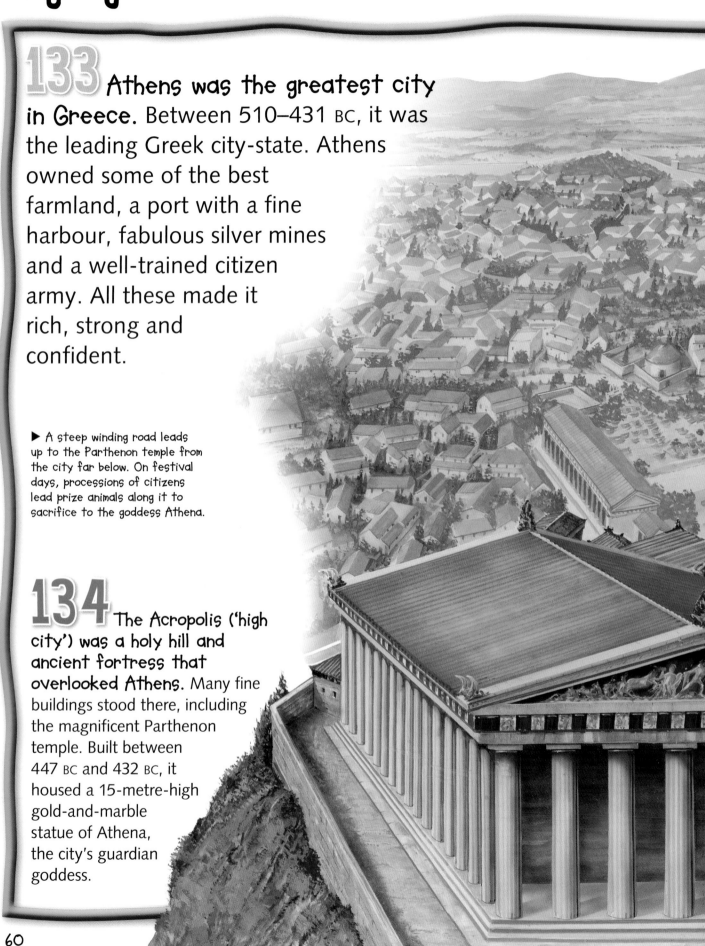

133 **Athens was the greatest city in Greece.** Between 510–431 BC, it was the leading Greek city-state. Athens owned some of the best farmland, a port with a fine harbour, fabulous silver mines and a well-trained citizen army. All these made it rich, strong and confident.

▶ A steep winding road leads up to the Parthenon temple from the city far below. On festival days, processions of citizens lead prize animals along it to sacrifice to the goddess Athena.

134 The Acropolis ('high city') was a holy hill and ancient fortress that overlooked Athens. Many fine buildings stood there, including the magnificent Parthenon temple. Built between 447 BC and 432 BC, it housed a 15-metre-high gold-and-marble statue of Athena, the city's guardian goddess.

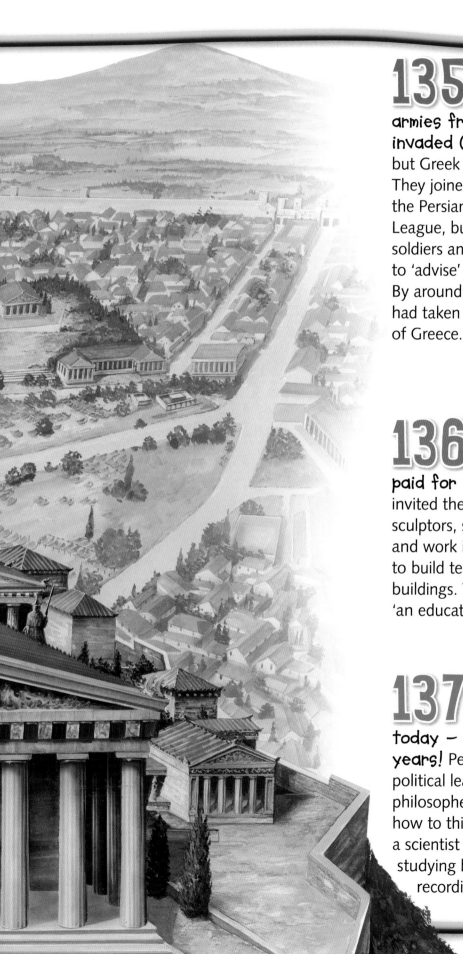

135 In 490 and 480 BC, armies from Persia (now Iran) invaded Greece. They were defeated, but Greek city-states felt threatened. They joined together in a League against the Persians. Athens took charge of the League, built a splendid navy and sent soldiers and government officials to 'advise' other city-states. By around 454 BC, Athens had taken control of most of Greece.

136 Athenian city leaders paid for fine works of art. They invited the best artists, architects, sculptors, scientists and scholars to live and work in their city, and gave money to build temples, monuments and public buildings. They vowed to make their city 'an education to Greece'.

137 Athenians are famous today — after more than 2000 years! Pericles was a great general and political leader. Socrates and Plato were philosophers and teachers who taught how to think and question. Aristotle was a scientist who pioneered a new way of studying by carefully observing and recording evidence.

Sparta

138 Sparta was Athens' great rival. It was a city-state set in wild mountain country in the far south of Greece. Sparta had kings who ruled together with a small elite group of citizens. Other Spartans were either free craftsmen who were not allowed to vote, or helots who had few rights but made up 80 percent of the population.

139 Sparta was always ready for war. Kings and citizens lived in fear that the helots might rebel. So all male Spartans had to train as warriors. After this, they were sent to live in barracks with other soldiers, ready to fight at any time.

140 The Spartans valued strength and toughness. When their sons were marching off to war Spartan women said "Come back carrying your shield (victorious) or carried on it (dead!)".

141 All Spartan citizens were warriors. Soldiers were famous for their bravery and loyalty – and for their bright red cloaks and long curling hair. Their main duty was to fight. They had no time to grow food, keep farm animals, build houses, make clothes or buy and sell. All these tasks, and more, were done by helot families.

▶ This bronze (metal) statue shows a Spartan girl running a race. Unlike other Greek women, she wears a short tunic and her hair is loose and free.

143
Women in Sparta were strong, like men. Young girls were made to do tough physical training. The Spartans believed this would make them grow up to produce strong, warlike sons. The girls were educated in reading and writing to the same level as the boys. Spartan women had to be emotionally tough as they spent most of their lives apart from their husbands and had to give up their children to serve the city-state.

142
Spartan children were trained to be tough. Citizen children were sent to state training camps. There, boys were treated very harshly so that they would learn to be tough and not complain. From seven years old they were taught to fight, kept cold and hungry and beaten so that they would learn to endure pain.

▶ The legendary toughness of Spartan warriors has inspired artists and film-makers. This scene, from the film 300, shows the Spartans' metal helmets, sharp spears and round shields.

War on land and sea

144 As teenagers, all Greek male citizens were trained to fight. They had to be ready to defend their city whenever danger threatened. City-states also employed men as bodyguards and mercenary troops with special skills.

▼▶ Soldiers had different duties. Cavalrymen were messengers and spies. Peltasts had to move fast and were armed with javelins. Mercenaries fought for anyone who would pay them.

Peltast

Cavalry

Hoplite

Mercenary

145 Each soldier paid for his own weapons and armour. Most soldiers were hoplites (soldiers who fought on foot). Their most important weapons were swords and spears. Poor men could not afford swords or armour. Their only weapons were slings for shooting stones and simple wooden spears.

146 Soldiers rarely fought on horseback. At the start of a battle, hoplites lined up side by side with their shields overlapping, like a wall. Then they marched towards the enemy while the peltasts threw their javelins. When they were close enough, the hoplites used their spears to fight the enemy.

◀ A Corinthian-style helmet. Soldiers tried to protect themselves from injury with bronze helmets, breastplates, greaves (shin guards) and round wooden shields.

ANCIENT GREECE

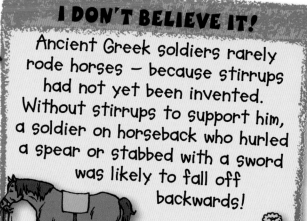

I DON'T BELIEVE IT!

Ancient Greek soldiers rarely rode horses — because stirrups had not yet been invented. Without stirrups to support him, a soldier on horseback who hurled a spear or stabbed with a sword was likely to fall off backwards!

▼ Greek ships were made of wood. If they were holed below the waterline they sank very quickly.

147 City-states paid for fleets of fast, fearsome wooden warships, called triremes. Each ship had a crew of about 170 oarsmen who sat in three sets of seats, one above the other. They rowed the ship as fast as they could towards enemy vessels, hoping that the sharp, pointed ram at its prow would smash or sink them. The most famous naval battle in Greece was fought at Salamis, near Athens, in 480 BC, when the Greeks defeated the Persians.

Farming and fishing

148 **Cities were surrounded by fields and farms.** Everyone living inside the walls relied on country people to grow crops, raise animals and bring food to sell at city markets. Some rich families owned country farms as well as city houses and workshops. They paid for servants or slaves to work the land for them.

▲ Satyrs (legendary monsters) picking and crushing ripe grapes to extract the juice to make wine.

149 **Farmers worked hard to make a living.** The climate was harsh and they had no big machines to help them. Men ploughed the soil, cut down trees, sheared sheep and harvested grain. Women milked sheep and goats, made cheese, grew vegetables, kept chickens and bees and gathered wild herbs and berries. Children scared birds from crops and watched over sheep and goats.

150 **Grain, grapes and olives were the most valuable crops.** Barley was the chief grain crop. It was used to make porridge or flour. Grapes were dried in the sun, or trampled by bare feet to extract the juice. This was turned into wine. Olives were crushed to produce oil. This was used in cooking, for burning in lamps or for cleaning and smoothing the skin.

▼ Sheep's wool was cleaned, combed, spun into thread then woven to make warm clothes, rugs and blankets.

151
The Greeks hunted in wild countryside. Mountains and steep valleys were covered in thick forests. Wild creatures lived there, such as wolves, bears, boar and deer. Huntsmen tracked and killed them for their skins or meat. They also trapped wild birds and stole eggs from their nests, and caught small creatures to eat such as hares and rabbits.

▶ A wild boar hunt (top) pictured on a Greek pot made around 600 BC.

152
Seaside communities made a living from fishing. Every day fishermen sailed out to catch tuna, mullet, squid, octopus and many other sea creatures. Villagers worked as boat-builders and sail-makers, or made ropes and fishing nets. Women prepared bait and preserved fish by drying or smoking to eat in winter.

▶ This wall painting from Minoan Crete shows a fisherman carrying home his catch of gleaming fresh fish.

153
Divers searched for sea produce to sell. They plunged deep underwater, holding their breath for as long as they could. They searched for shellfish (to eat and use as dye for cloth) and sponges, which the Greeks used when bathing. Sponges were also useful for doctors – they soaked up blood.

▼ A modern display of Greek seafood. Fish and shellfish might have been even better in ancient Greek times because the Mediterranean Sea was less polluted.

Food and drink

154 Greek food was plain, hearty and healthy. It included whole grains, cheese, beans and lentils, fruits, vegetables, olives and for special occasions – a little meat or fish.

► Preparing a meal in an open-air kitchen in the courtyard of a house. Food was cooked over a wood fire in a stone hearth.

Mixing barley and honey to make cakes

Oil and wine stored in jars

Slabs of stone or pottery tiles for floor

All the cooking was done by hand

Stone hearth with metal racks for cooking

155 Main meals were breakfast and dinner. Breakfast was bread dipped in olive oil or stale wine. Dinner was olives, then eggs, dried bean stew or hot barley porridge. This was followed by vegetables, fruit and honeycomb. Some people ate a light lunch of bread with fruit or cheese.

▼ A pottery bowl decorated with tasty-looking fish.

156 Greek cooking was very simple. Boiling, stewing or grilling were the only methods of cooking. Many foods were eaten raw, such as fruit, herbs and some shellfish. The Greeks disapproved of cooked dishes with lots of different ingredients, saying that they were too indulgent.

Cooking pots
stored on
wooden shelf

Walls of rough
plaster

157 The Greeks enjoyed wine – but always mixed it with water. Wine could be rough, strong and unsuitable for drinking. People also thought that drunkenness was shameful, except at parties for men only. They did not want to see their guests disgracing themselves.

158 There might be hungry months in winter. Meals were based on preserved foods and grain from the summer harvest. If these ran out or decayed, families went hungry. The only food preservation techniques were smoking, pickling, steeping in olive oil or drying in the sun.

159 Dinner parties were for men only. When husbands invited their male friends to a symposion (dinner party), their wives and daughters stayed away. At a party, male diners reclined on couches while slaves served food and wine.

Table of
scrubbed wood

160 A Greek dinner party might go on for hours and hours. Guests discussed sport and politics, listened to music, played silly games – and sometimes fell asleep between courses!

Family life

161
Families were very important. A person's wealth, rank and occupation all depended on their family circumstances, as did the part they played in community life. Some families were very active in politics and had powerful friends – and enemies.

163
All Greek parents longed for a son. Boys passed on the family name to the next generation and they could protect family property and run businesses or farms. However, girls had to be fed and housed at the family's expense, then they left to get married.

Bedrooms were upstairs

Pottery tiles

Mud-brick walls covered with plaster

Slaves cooked in the kitchen

Prayers were said around the altar each morning

162
Fathers were the heads of families. They had power over everyone in their households – wives, children and slaves. However, families also worked as a team to find food, make a safe, comfortable home and train their children in all the skills they would need in adult life.

▲ Greek houses were designed to provide security and privacy. They had high, windowless outer walls and a hidden inner courtyard, which only the inhabitants and trusted visitors could see.

164 Most girls married very young, aged around 13 years. Their husbands, who were several years older, were chosen by their fathers for political or business reasons. A marriage linked two families together. Romantic love was not important in marriage – the Greeks thought it was dangerous!

▼ Weddings took place at dusk. The bride was driven to the bridegroom's family home, accompanied by guests carrying flaming wooden torches.

165 Women did not have the same rights as men. Many women had strong opinions about city and community life. A few were also well-educated and interested in the latest ideas. However, according to the law, women could not vote, make a public speech or take any part in politics.

166 Funerals were important family occasions. Wives and daughters spent most of their lives at home but they were allowed to attend family funerals. All family members said prayers together and made offerings to the gods in memory of the dead person.

Education

167 From their earliest days, children were expected to play their part in the family. This meant being well-behaved, obedient, sharing family worship of the gods and showing respect to their parents.

▲ A schoolroom scene, pictured on a Greek pot, showing a music lesson, a writing lesson and a slave. The slave is there to make sure that his master's son behaves and works hard.

168 From around seven years old, boys from wealthy families went to school. They learnt reading, writing, simple arithmetic, how to sing or play a musical instrument and how to debate and recite poetry. They also practised favourite Greek sports such as running, jumping, wrestling and throwing the javelin.

169
School was not for girls. They stayed at home and learned skills such as spinning, weaving and cookery. Wealthy women taught their daughters how to read and write, keep accounts, manage a big household and give orders. Older women also passed on traditional songs and dances so that girls could take part in religious festivals.

▲ This statue shows a slave girl mixing flour, yeast and water to make bread.

170
Socrates was a scholar and teacher who lived in Athens. He encouraged his students to try to discover the truth by asking careful, thoughtful questions. However, his constant questioning alarmed political leaders who accused him of misleading young people. Socrates was condemned to death by the Athens law courts and given poison. He died in 399 BC.

171
Most boys left school when they were 14 years old. Older boys might study with local scholars or sophists (travelling teachers). Around 380 BC, a man called Plato opened a study centre in Athens called the Academy. He planned to train young men to work for the city-state, but attracted the best students in Greece who became famous for their brilliant ideas.

▶ Plato believed that thinking and learning were essential for a good life.

Clothes and fashion

172
Greek clothes were just draped around the body. They were loose and flowing, for comfort in the hot summer months. For extra warmth in winter, both men and women draped a thick woolly himation (cloak) over their shoulders.

▶ Men's clothing was designed for action. Young men wore short tunics so they could work – and fight – easily. Older men's robes were longer.

173
Each piece of cloth used to make a garment was specially made. It had to be the right length and width to fit the wearer. All cloth was handwoven, usually by women in their homes. Cool, smooth linen was the favourite cloth for summer. In winter, Greeks preferred cosy wool. Very rich people wore fine clothes of silk imported from India.

◀ Women's clothing was modest and draped the body from top to toe. Respectable women covered their heads and faces with a veil when they went outside the house.

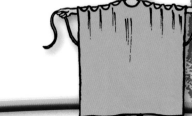

MAKE A GREEK CHITON

You will need:
length of cloth twice as wide as your outstretched arms and half your height
safety pins   belt or length of cord

1. Fold the cloth in half.

2. Fasten two edges of the cloth together with safety pins, leaving a gap of about 30 cm in the middle.

3. Pull the cloth over your head so that the safety pins sit on your shoulders.

4. Fasten the belt or cord around your waist. Pull some of the cloth over the belt so that the cloth is level with your knees.

174

Women – and men – took care of their skin. To keep their skin smooth and supple, men and women rubbed themselves all over with olive oil. Rich women also used sunshades or face powder to achieve a fashionably pale complexion. They did not want to look sun-tanned – that was for farm workers, slaves – and men!

Before 500 BC

500–300 BC

After 300 BC

▲ Before 500 BC, long, natural hairstyles were popular. Between 500–300 BC, women tied their hair up and held it in place with ribbons or scarves. After 300 BC, curled styles and jewelled hair ornaments were popular and men shaved off their beards.

175

Curls were very fashionable. Women grew their hair long and tied it up with ribbons or headbands, leaving long curls trailing over their shoulders. Men, except for Spartan warriors, had short curly hair. Male and female slaves had their hair cropped very short – this was a shameful sign.

176

The Greeks liked to look good and admired fit, slim, healthy bodies. Women were praised for their grace and beauty. Young men were admired for their strong figures, and often went without clothes when training for war or taking part in sports competitions. Top athletes became celebrities, and were asked by artists to pose for them as models.

◄ Athletes and their trainer (left) pictured on a Greek vase.

177

Sponges, showers and swimming helped the Greeks keep clean. Most houses did not have piped water. So people washed themselves by standing under waterfalls, swimming in streams or squeezing a big sponge full of water over their heads, like a shower.

Gods and goddesses

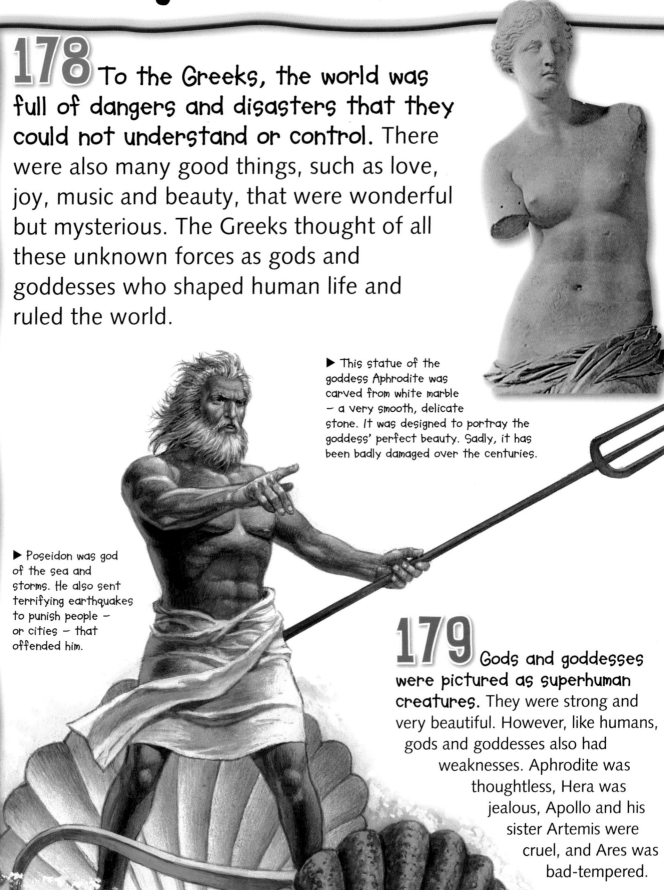

178 To the Greeks, the world was full of dangers and disasters that they could not understand or control. There were also many good things, such as love, joy, music and beauty, that were wonderful but mysterious. The Greeks thought of all these unknown forces as gods and goddesses who shaped human life and ruled the world.

▶ This statue of the goddess Aphrodite was carved from white marble – a very smooth, delicate stone. It was designed to portray the goddess' perfect beauty. Sadly, it has been badly damaged over the centuries.

▶ Poseidon was god of the sea and storms. He also sent terrifying earthquakes to punish people – or cities – that offended him.

179 Gods and goddesses were pictured as superhuman creatures. They were strong and very beautiful. However, like humans, gods and goddesses also had weaknesses. Aphrodite was thoughtless, Hera was jealous, Apollo and his sister Artemis were cruel, and Ares was bad-tempered.

▲ Odysseus and his shipmates were surrounded by the Sirens – beautiful half-women, half-bird monsters. They sang sweet songs, calling sailors towards dangerous rocks where their ships were wrecked.

180 The Greeks believed in magic spirits and monsters.

These included Gorgons who turned men to stone, and Sirens – bird-women whose song lured sailors to their doom. They also believed in witchcraft and curses and tried to fight against them. People painted magic eyes on the prows of their ships to keep a look-out for evil.

181 Individuals were often anxious to see what the future would bring.

They believed that oracles (holy messengers) could see the future. The most famous oracles were at Delphi, where a drugged priestess answered questions, and at Dodona, where the leaves of sacred trees whispered words from the gods.

▶ Herakles was a hero – a man who became a god. He performed amazing feats of strength and fought against many monsters. This statue shows him killing a centaur, half-man, half-horse.

182 Poets and dramatists retold myths and legends about the gods.

Some stories were explanations of natural events – thunder was the god Zeus shaking his fist in anger. Others explored bad thoughts and feelings shared by gods and humans, such as greed and disloyalty.

Temples and festivals

183 In Greece and the lands where the Greeks settled, we can still see remains of huge, beautiful temples. They were built as holy homes for gods and goddesses. Each city-state had its own guardian god and many temples housed a huge, lifelike statue of him or her. People hoped that the god's spirit might visit them and live in the statue for a while.

▶ This gigantic statue of the goddess Athena was 15 metres high and was made of gold and ivory. It stood inside her finest temple, the Parthenon in Athens. In her right hand, Athena holds Nike, the goddess of victory.

184 As well as visiting a temple, people hoped – or feared – that they might meet a god or goddess in a forest or on a mountain top. It was thought that all the gods met at Mount Olympus to feast, love, quarrel and make plans. Another high peak, Mount Parnassus, was sacred to the Muses – nine graceful goddesses who guided the arts, such as music and drama.

▲ The summit of the tallest mountain in Greece, Mount Olympus (1951 metres), was often hidden in clouds. It was remote, dangerous and mysterious – a suitable home for the mighty gods.

▼ The first temples were made of wood and shaped like ordinary houses. By around 600 BC, temples were built of stone.

185 People offered prayers and sacrifices (gifts) to their gods and goddesses. Gifts might be just a few drops of wine or a valuable live animal. The meat of the sacrifice was cooked and shared among the worshippers and the bones and skin were burned on the altar. People thought that smoke carried their prayers up to the gods.

c. 800 BC tree trunks hold up the roof. Small inner room.

c. 600 BC tree trunks replaced by stone columns. More rooms inside.

186 City-states held festivals to honour their guardian gods. There would be a procession towards the city's main temple or to a shrine (holy place). At temples, crowds watched priests and priestesses making special sacrifices. At shrines, citizens might take part in secret rituals. Afterwards there could be music and drama or sports contests.

c. 440 BC temples are huge, with rows of columns and carved decorations.

Olympic Games

187 The Olympic Games began as a festival to honour Zeus. Over the centuries, it grew into the greatest sports event in the Greek world. A huge festival complex was built at Olympia with a temple, sports tracks, seats for 40,000 spectators, a campsite and rooms for visitors and a field full of stalls selling food and drink.

▶ Victory! The Greeks believed that winners were chosen by the gods. The first known Olympic Games was held in 776 BC, though the festival may have begun years earlier.

188 Every four years athletes travelled from all over Greece to take part in the Olympic Games. They had to obey strict rules – respect for Zeus, no fights among competitors and no weapons anywhere near the sports tracks. In return they claimed protection – the holy Olympic Peace. Anyone who attacked them on their journeys was severely punished.

QUIZ

1. When was the first Olympic Games held?
2. Could women go to the Olympic Games?
3. What did winning athletes wear on their heads?

Answers:
1. 776 BC, though the festival may have begun years earlier 2. No. There was a separate women's games held 3. Crowns of holy laurel leaves

189
The most popular events were running, long jump, wrestling and boxing. Spectators might also watch chariot races, athletes throwing the discus and javelin or weightlifting contests. The most prestigious event was the 200-metre sprint. There was also a dangerous fighting contest called *pankration* (total power).

▲ Boxers did not wear gloves. Instead they wrapped their hands in bandages.

190
Many events featured weapons or skills that were needed in war. One of the most gruelling competitions was a race wearing heavy battle armour. The main Olympic Games were for men only – women could not take part. There was a separate women's games held at Olympia on different years from the men's competitions.

▲ Throwing the discus was a test of strength and balance. It was also useful training for war.

▲ Swimmer Michael Phelps sets a new world record at the Beijing Olympics, 2008. The modern Olympics is modelled on the ancient games and since 1896 has remained the world's greatest sports festival.

191
Athletes who won Olympic contests were honoured as heroes. They were crowned with wreaths of holy laurel leaves and given valuable prizes of olive oil, fine clothes and pottery. Poets composed songs in their praise and their home city-states often rewarded them with free food and lodgings for life!

▶ A crown of laurel leaves was given to winning athletes as a sign of their god-like strength and speed.

Plays and poems

192 Greek drama originated at religious festivals. In the earliest rituals, priests and priestesses sometimes played the part of gods or goddesses. They acted out stories told about them or famous local heroes. Over the years, these ancient rituals changed into a new art form – drama.

193 Drama became so popular that many city-states built splendid new open-air theatres. Greek theatres were built in a half-circle shape with tiers (raised rows) of seats looking down over an open space for performers. Most seats were filled by men – women were banned from many plays.

194 All the parts in a play were performed by men. They wore masks, wigs and elaborate costumes to look like women or magic spirits and monsters. Some theatres had ladders and cranes so that actors playing gods could appear to fly or sit among the clouds.

▶ The theatre at Epidaurus, in southern Greece, is one of the largest built by the ancient Greeks. It had seats for over 10,000 spectators.

195
In some city-states, especially Athens, drama remained an important part of several religious festivals. Writers competed for prizes for the best new plays. They wrote serious plays called tragedies and lively comedies. Some plays lasted all day long. Others had extra 'satyr plays' added on. These were short, funny pieces.

196
Music for poetry was played on a lyre. This was rather like a small harp, but had a real (dead) hollow tortoise shell as a sounding-box!

▼ Actors wore masks to show which character they were playing. Bright-coloured masks were for cheerful characters and dark-coloured masks were more gloomy. Some masks were double-sided so that the actors could change parts quickly.

197
Plays were written like poetry. The main actors were always accompanied by singers and dancers. Poems were also recited to music. Tunes were sad for tragic poems or rousing for those about war. Poets performed at men's dinner parties and in rich families' homes. Public storytellers entertained crowds by singing poems in the streets.

Barbarian – or monster – with wild, shaggy hair

Angry young man

Huge, funnel-shaped mouths helped the actors' words reach the audience

Masks with beards and bald heads were for actors playing old men

Scientists and thinkers

198 The Greeks liked to ask questions and discuss things. Although they believed in gods and magic, they also wanted to investigate the world in a practical way. Some mathematics and astronomy was learned from the Egyptians and Babylonians. Then the Greeks used this knowledge to find out more for themselves.

▶ Hipparchus (170–126 BC) observed and recorded the position of over 800 stars and worked out a way of measuring their brightness.

I DON'T BELIEVE IT!

Pythagoras' followers believed in reincarnation (being born again in a different body). They were vegetarians — but they would not eat beans because they might contain reborn human souls.

199 Mathematicians and astronomers made important discoveries. Aristarchus was the first to understand that the Earth travels around the Sun. Hipparchus mapped the stars. Thales discovered mathematical laws about circles and triangles. Pythagoras worked out the mathematics behind music and measured the movements of the Sun and the Moon.

200
Many people believed that illness was a punishment sent by the gods. However doctors, led by Hippocrates (460–370 BC), tried to cure people with good food, fresh air, exercise and herbal medicines. They carefully observed patients for signs of illness and recorded the results of their prescriptions. That way they could prove scientifically which treatments worked best for each disease.

▼ Archimedes was the most famous Greek engineer. He invented (or improved) a spiral pump to make water flow uphill, for example, from rivers into fields.

Handle turns wooden screw

Water is lifted round and round and then pushed out

Water is pulled in as the screw turns

▲ This stone carving shows a doctor treating an injured arm. Greek doctors were some of the first in the world to treat patients scientifically.

201
Engineers designed many clever machines. Speakers at the Athenian Assembly were timed by a water-powered clock and there were machines that used hot air to open temple doors. Archimedes (287–211 BC) discovered how objects float and balance. He also designed a 'sun gun' (huge glass lens) to focus the Sun's rays on enemy ships to set them on fire.

202
Greek thinkers thought about thinking! As well as investigating the world and creating new inventions they also wanted to understand people and society. They asked questions such as 'How do we think?', 'How do we see and feel?', 'What is good?' and 'How can we live the best lives?'.

ANCIENT ROME

River Tiber
This was a source of water for the people of Rome

Circus Maximus
A huge stadium built to stage public entertainment

Imperial Palace
First built around AD 30 the palace remained in use for 300 years

Temple of the Divine Claudius
A temple dedicated to the patron gods of the imperial family

203 The Italian city of Rome was once the hub of one of the world's greatest empires. An empire is made up of lots of countries governed by one ruler. Around 1000 BC Rome was a village on the River Tiber, but it soon grew rich and powerful. It was busy and exciting, with many beautiful buildings. By 200 BC the Romans ruled most of Italy, and started to invade neighbouring lands.

Forum
The political and business centre of the empire

Temple of Apollo
The Greek god Apollo became popular in Rome in later years

Colosseum
Famous amphitheatre where gladiatorial fights were staged

Baths of Trajan
Built by the Emperor Trajan as a place of relaxation for citizens

Ludus Magnus
Training school and barracks for gladiators who fought in the Colosseum

Servian Wall
The stone wall around Rome built around 490 BC. It was replaced by the larger Aurelian Wall in about AD 275 and was allowed to fall into ruin

Aqua Claudia
Aqueduct that brought fresh water to Rome from springs 72 kilometres to the southeast

▲ The Forum was the central hub of Rome. It was the home of government and a busy marketplace. The rest of the city contained places for leisure, sport and religion, and was filled with houses and blocks of flats where the citizens lived.

Capital city

204 **Over one million people lived in Rome.** By around AD 300, Rome was the largest city in the world. There were citizens who could vote and serve in the army, and there were non-citizens who did not have these rights. The government was run by wealthy nobles and knights. Plebeians (ordinary people) were usually fairly poor but were citizens of Rome. Slaves were non-citizens. They were not free to leave their owners and had no rights.

▼ In 44 BC the dictator Julius Caesar built the Curia Julia as a meeting house for the Senate of Rome. The building later became a church and has survived intact to the present day.

205 **The Forum was the centre of Rome.** It was originally an open space at the foot of the Capitoline Hill, and was used as a market place, meeting place and picnic area. Later, government buildings were erected here, including offices for the Senate, law courts and temples.

Aurelian Wall

Servian Wall

206
Rome was very well protected. It was surrounded by 50 kilometres of strong stone walls to keep out attackers. Visitors had to enter the city through one of its 37 gates, which were guarded by soldiers and watchmen.

◀ In AD 275 the old Servian Wall of about 380 BC was replaced by the Aurelian Wall that protected the new, larger city of Rome. The new wall was 19 kilometres long, 16 metres tall and had 383 towers. It remained in use until the siege of 1870.

208
Rome relied on its drains. The city was so crowded that without good drains the citizens could have caught diseases from sewage and died. The largest sewer, called the *cloaca maxima*, was so high and wide that a horse and cart could drive through it.

I DON'T BELIEVE IT!
Roman engineers also designed public lavatories. They were convenient but not at all private — users had to sit on rows of seats, side by side!

207
The Romans were great water engineers. They designed aqueducts (raised channels to carry water from streams in distant hills and mountains to the city). The homes of rich citizens were supplied with running water carried in lead pipes. Ordinary people had to drink from public fountains.

▶ The Romans built the Pont Du Gard in the south of France — a 360-metre-long aqueduct supported on three tiers of arches.

Roman homes

▲ A reconstruction of a house belonging to a rich family in the city of Pompeii. This grand room, the Atrium, was where guests were entertained.

QUIZ

1. What were Roman blocks of flats known as?
2. What are pictures made with coloured stones or glass called?
3. How did Romans heat their homes?

Answers:
1. *Insulae* 2. Mosaics 3. Wealthy families had underfloor heating, ordinary families used fires

209 **Rich Romans had more than one home.** Rome was noisy, dirty and smelly. Wealthy citizens would often have a house just outside the city (a *villa urbana*), or a big house with land in the country (a *villa rustica*) in which they spent the summer months.

210

The Romans built the world's first high-rise apartments. Most of the people who lived in Ostia, a busy port close to Rome, had jobs connected with trade, such as shipbuilders and money-changers. They lived in blocks of flats known as *insulae*. A typical block was three or four storeys high, with up to 100 small, dirty, crowded rooms.

▼ On the ground floor of an *insula* were shops, and on the first floor were flats and apartments for families. The poorest families lived in single rooms on the top floor.

212

Many homes had a pool, but it wasn't used for swimming! Decorative pools were built in the central courtyards of large homes, surrounded by plants and statues. Some had fountains. In others mosaics (pictures made of tiny coloured stones or squares of glass) covered the floor.

213

Rome's fire brigade was made up of specially trained freed slaves. People who could not afford central heating warmed their rooms with fires in clay pots, which often set houses alight.

Space in walls for hot air to circulate

211

Wealthy family homes had underfloor central heating. Blasts of hot air, warmed by a wood-burning furnace, circulated in channels built beneath the floor. Slaves chopped wood and stoked the fire.

▶ Some public buildings and wealthy homes had a heating system called a hypocaust. Hot air from a fire tended by a slave passed through spaces under the floor and up the walls to keep the rooms warm.

Fire in basement

Space under floor for hot air to circulate

Buying and selling

214 Roman ships travelled the known world. Merchants sailed around the Empire and beyond looking for trade. Ships reached as far as India to the east and Iceland to the north. Luxury goods, such as silk, spices and furs, were the most sought after.

QUIZ

1. How many levels was Trajan's Market built on?
2. Who wore jewellery in ancient Rome – men or women?
3. Did Roman ships sail to Iceland?

Answers:
1. Five 2. Both men and women wore jewellery 3. Yes – they sailed there to trade

▼ A Roman ship approaches Dubris (now Dover) in Britain in AD 90 as a lighthouse is built on the cliff to help guide ships into harbour.

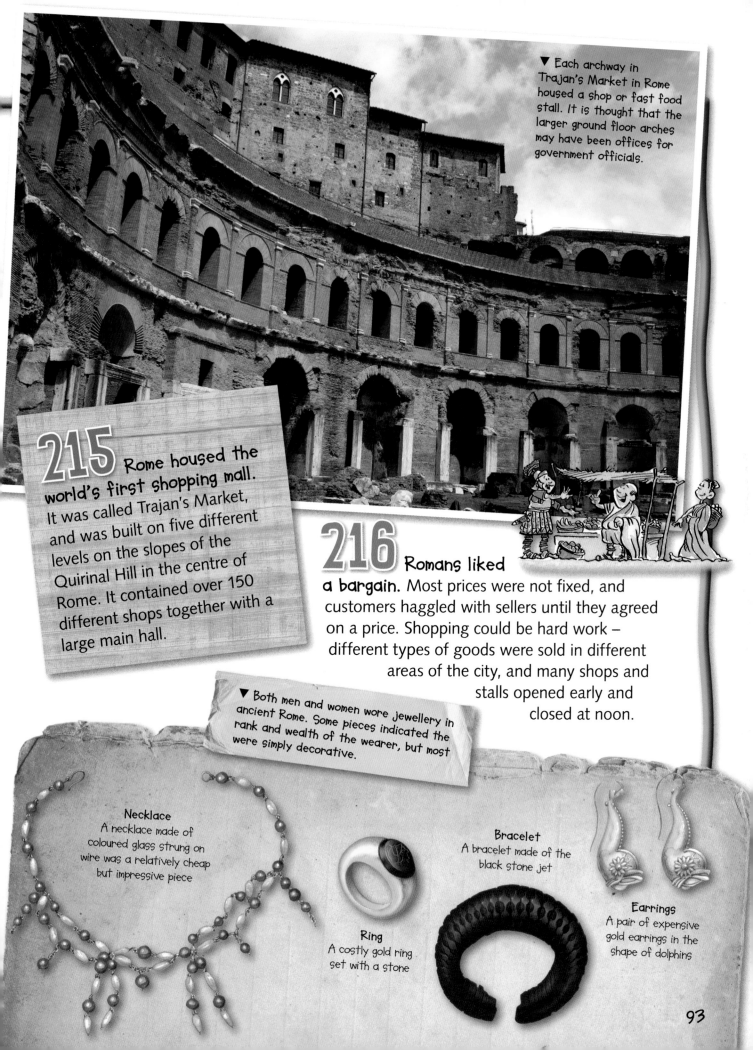

▼ Each archway in Trajan's Market in Rome housed a shop or fast food stall. It is thought that the larger ground floor arches may have been offices for government officials.

215 Rome housed the world's first shopping mall. It was called Trajan's Market, and was built on five different levels on the slopes of the Quirinal Hill in the centre of Rome. It contained over 150 different shops together with a large main hall.

216 Romans liked a bargain. Most prices were not fixed, and customers haggled with sellers until they agreed on a price. Shopping could be hard work – different types of goods were sold in different areas of the city, and many shops and stalls opened early and closed at noon.

▼ Both men and women wore jewellery in ancient Rome. Some pieces indicated the rank and wealth of the wearer, but most were simply decorative.

Necklace
A necklace made of coloured glass strung on wire was a relatively cheap but impressive piece

Ring
A costly gold ring set with a stone

Bracelet
A bracelet made of the black stone jet

Earrings
A pair of expensive gold earrings in the shape of dolphins

93

Eating and drinking

217 Most Romans ate little during the day. They had bread and water for breakfast and a snack of bread, cheese or fruit around midday. The main meal was eaten in the late afternoon, and in rich households it had three courses. Poor people ate simple food: soups made with lentils and onions, barley porridge, peas, cabbage and cheap cuts of meat stewed in vinegar.

▲ Romans ate large quantities of fruit raw, cooked or dried. Grapes were crushed and made into wine.

Grapes

Figs

ROMAN FOOD

Patina de piris (Pear soufflé)

Ingredients:

1 kg pears (peeled and cored)
6 eggs (beaten)   4 tbsp honey
oil   pinch of salt   ½ tsp cumin
ground pepper to taste

Ask an adult to help you with this recipe. Mash the pears together with the pepper, cumin, honey, and a bit of oil. Add the beaten eggs and put into a casserole dish. Cook for approximately 30 minutes in a moderate oven. Serve with a little pepper sprinkled on top.

▶ An engraved drinking cup made in Gaul, France, in about AD 380. The skills of making glass were lost after the fall of Rome.

218 Only rich people had their own kitchen. They could afford to employ a chef with slaves to help him. Ordinary people went to *popinae* (cheap eating houses) for their main meal, or bought ready-cooked snacks from roadside fast food stalls.

▲ Herbs and spices added flavour to dishes. Pepper and coriander came from across the Indian Ocean and were very expensive.

Oregano

Black pepper

Juniper berries

Coriander seeds

Thyme

Garlic

Olives

Asparagus

Lentils

Radishes

Celery

▲ Vegetables were eaten raw or cooked in stews. Garlic was a favourite ingredient used in many dishes.

Sardine

▲ Fish and meat were relatively expensive so poorer people rarely ate them. Sardines could be dried and salted for storage.

219 At parties, the Romans ate lying down. Men and women lay on long couches arranged around a table. They also often wore crowns of flowers, and took off their sandals before entering the dining room.

▼ A relief shows a rich woman reclining on a couch with her child while a slave or servant brings in a dish of food.

School days

220 Roman boys learned to speak well. At school they were taught reading, maths and public speaking – skills they would need in their careers. There were no newspapers or TVs, so politicians, army leaders and government officials had to make speeches to explain their plans and policies to Roman crowds.

▼ Boys attended school from seven years old. At 16, their education was complete.

221 Roman girls did not go to school. They stayed at home, where their mothers or women slaves taught them household tasks, such as how to cook, clean, weave cloth and look after children. Girls from wealthy families, or families who ran a business, also learned to read, write and keep accounts.

222 Many of the best teachers were slaves. Schoolmasters and private tutors often came from Greece. They were purchased by wealthy people who wanted to give their sons a good education. The Greeks had a long tradition of learning, which the Romans admired.

▼ An inscription in Latin placed over the doorway of a house. It means 'Peace to those coming in'.

PAX · INTRANTIBVS
SALVS · EXEVNTIBVS

223 **The Romans did not write on paper.** They used thin slices of wood for letters and day-to-day business. For notes Romans used flat, wooden boards covered with wax, as the wax could be smoothed over and used again. For important documents that they wanted to keep, they used cleaned, polished calfskin or papyrus.

Ink pot

Pens

Stylus, to use with a wax tablet

Wax tablet

R

224 **Romans made ink from soot.** Black ink was a mixture of soot, vinegar and a sticky gum that oozed from tree bark. Some Roman writing has survived for almost 2000 years.

▶ A list of Roman words and their English meanings. Some modern words are based on Roman words. For instance the word 'library' comes from *liber*.

ROMAN	ENGLISH
EPISTOLA	LETTER
VELLUM	CALFSKIN
GRAMMATICUS	SCHOOLMASTER
PAEDAGOGUS	PRIVATE TUTOR
STYLUS	WRITING STICK
BIBLIOTHECA	LIBRARY
LIBER	BOOK
LIBRARII	SLAVES WHO WORKED IN A LIBRARY

▲ Quick notes were scribbled on a wax tablet and wiped clean later. More important messages were written in ink onto vellum (calfskin parchment).

226 **Many Romans read standing up.** It took time and patience to learn how to read from a papyrus scroll. Most were at least 10 metres long. Readers held the scroll in their right hand, a stick in their left, and unrolled a small section of the scroll at a time.

225 **Many boys did not go to school.** Poorer boys who needed to earn a living would get a job in a workshop or on a farm. They learned how to run a business or carry out a trade. At 16 they might set up in business on their own.

In the family

227 A Roman father had the power of life and death over his family. By law each family was led by a man – usually the oldest surviving male. He was known as the *paterfamilias* (father of a family). The house and its contents belonged to him. He had the right to punish any family members who misbehaved – even his mother and other older female relatives.

▶ A Roman wedding. The bride and groom hold hands while their families watch. Most marriages were arranged by the families for business or political reasons. The couple being married had little say in the decision.

228 Families included more than blood relations. To the Romans, the word 'family' meant all the people living and working together in the same household. So families included many different slaves and servants, as well as a husband, wife and their children.

◀ The Romans gave a good luck charm, called a *bulla*, to their babies.

I DON'T BELIEVE IT!

The Romans invented Valentine's Day, but called it Lupercalia. Boys picked a girl's name from a hat, and she was meant to be their girlfriend for the year!

229 Life in Rome was easier if you were a boy. Boys were valued because they would carry on the family name, and might bring fame and honour to a family through their careers. For Roman girls, childhood was short. They were often married by the age of 12, and many had become mothers by the time they were 15.

230 Families liked to keep pets. Many statues and paintings show children playing with animals. Dogs, cats and doves were all popular. Some families also kept ornamental fish and tame deer.

▶ Roman women play with a fawn (young deer), while enjoying a day in the countryside.

231 Funerals were very elaborate. A funeral was a chance for a family to show off to their friends and neighbours. Huge feasts were provided, speeches were made and actors played out incidents from the life of the dead person.

◀ Some Romans cremated their dead. The ashes were then put in an urn before being buried, often in a family tomb.

Roman style

232 Most Roman clothes were made without sewing. Loose-fitting robes made of long strips of cloth were draped round the body and held in place by pins, brooches or belts. Most women wore layers – a *tunica* (thin shift), a *stola* (long, sleeveless dress), and a *palla* (cloak). Men wore a *colobium* (knee-length tunic) with a semi-circular cloak called a toga over the top.

▶ Three different ways that women could wear the *palla*, which was often made of costly fabric.

233 Clothes were different depending on how important you were. Ordinary men wore plain white togas, but government leaders, called senators, appeared in togas with a purple stripe around the edge. Rich men and women wore robes made of smooth, fine-quality wool and silk. Ordinary people's clothes were much rougher.

◀ This mosaic shows a man wearing a toga. The toga could be worn only by men who were citizens of Rome. Many men had a special toga of costly coloured linen to wear at special events.

▶ A gold fibula, or pin. These small pins were used to hold cloaks and tunics in place.

234

Clothes told the world who you were. People from many different cultures lived in lands ruled by Rome, and they wore different styles of clothes. Men from Egypt wore wigs and linen kilts. Celtic women from northern Europe wore long, woollen shawls, woven in brightly coloured checks. Celtic men wore trousers.

TOGA TIME!

1. Ask an adult for a blanket or sheet. White is best, like the Romans.
2. Drape the sheet over your left shoulder. Now pass the rest behind your back.
3. Pull the sheet across your front, so that you're wrapped up in it.
4. Finally, drape the last end over your right hand and there you have it, a Roman toga!

◀ Sandals known as *crepidae* were worn by men and women all year round.

235

Boots were made for walking! Soldiers and travellers wore lace-up boots with thick leather soles studded with iron nails. Other footwear included *socci*, loose-fitting slippers to wear indoors. Farmers wore shoes made of a single piece of ox-hide wrapped round the foot, called *carbatinae*. There were also *crepidae* – comfortable lace-up sandals with open toes.

▲ These Roman sandals have metal studs in the soles to make sure that they don't wear down too quickly.

Bath time

▼ The Roman baths at Bath, in Somerset. Only the actual water bath is original, the other buildings date from the 18th century.

236 The Romans went to public baths to relax. These huge buildings were more than just places to get clean. They were also fitness centres and meeting places. Visitors could take part in sports, such as wrestling, do exercises, have a massage or a haircut. They could buy scented oils and perfumes, read books, eat snacks or admire works of art in the bath's own sculpture gallery!

237 Men and women could not bathe together. Women usually went to the baths in the mornings, while most men were at work. Men went to the baths in the afternoons.

238 Although the Romans liked bathing, they visited the baths only once in every nine days. Basins of water were used in between baths to wash hands or faces.

239 **Bathing wasn't simple – there were lots of stages.** First bathers sat in a very hot room full of steam. Then they went into a hot, dry room, where a slave removed all the sweat and dirt from their skin, using a metal scraper and olive oil. To cool off, they went for a swim in a tepid pool. Finally, they jumped into a bracing cold pool.

▼ The Baths of Caracalla in Rome included not only baths but libraries, shops and gardens that covered a total of 25 hectares.

② *Tepidarium*
Cool or tepid pool

① *Caldarium*
Hot room

③ *Frigidarium*
Coldest pool

Fires heat the water for the hot rooms

▲ Roman baths were open to anyone who paid the entrance fee. They were one of the few areas where rich and poor mixed freely. Some baths had two sections, one for men and one for women, but most baths had days for men and days for women.

Having fun

240 Roman theatre-goers preferred comedies to tragedies. Comic plays had happy endings, and made audiences laugh. Tragedies were serious, and ended with misery and suffering. The Romans also liked clowns, and invented mime, a story told without words, through dance and movement.

▼ All the parts in Roman plays were performed by men. For women's roles, men wore masks and dressed in female costume. Women could not be actors, except in mime.

Stages were backed by permanent walls of stone with doorways and balconies that could be used to represent temples and houses

The front of the stage was called the *pulpitum*. Actors stood here to make important speeches

Theatres had no roofs, so audiences were not undercover. Plays took place only during the day when there was enough light

QUIZ

1. What is the name for a story told through dance and music without words?

2. Why did some Roman politicians give away free tickets to plays?

3. How many people could be seated in the Roman theatre at Orange in France?

Answers:
1. Mime 2. In the hope of winning votes 3. 10,000

241 Plays were originally part of religious festivals. Many dramas showed scenes from myths and legends, and were designed to make people think about morals. Later, plays were written on all sorts of topics – including politics. Some were paid for by rich politicians, to spread their message. They gave free tickets to Roman citizens, hoping to win votes.

242 Theatres were huge and well-built. The theatre at Orange in France seats almost 10,000 people and is so cleverly designed that even people in the back row can hear the actors.

Seats were made of hard stone, but sometimes people could hire soft cushions to sit on

243 Actors wore masks to help audiences see what each character was feeling. They were carved and painted in bright colours, with large features and exaggerated expressions of happiness, sadness or fright.

244 The Romans liked music and dancing. Groups of buskers played in the streets, or could be hired for parties. Among ordinary families, favourite instruments included pipes, castanets, flutes, cymbals and horns. Rich, educated people preferred the gentler sound of the lyre, which was played to accompany poets and singers.

245 People enjoyed games of skill and chance. Adults and children played dice and knucklebones, which needed nimble fingers. They played a game similar to draughts, which relied on luck and quick thinking. Sometimes bets were made on who would win.

▶ Six-sided dice were made of bone or ivory. They were shaken in a round pot before being thrown.

◀ Masks worn by Roman actors as shown in a mosaic from Rome. The male mask was used for comedy, the female for tragedy.

Let the games begin

246 Gladiators were admired for their strength, skill and bravery. These men were sent into an arena (an open space with tiered seats on all sides) to fight. Most gladiators would be killed or badly injured in the arena.

▶ Different types of gladiator had special equipment and fought in ways governed by strict rules, which were enforced by a referee.

Secutor

Samnite

Hoplomachus

247 Most gladiators didn't choose to fight. They were prisoners of war or criminals condemned to fight in the arena. Some men volunteered as gladiators to gain fame and wealth. Success could bring riches and freedom.

248 A gladiator who won a fight would be rewarded with a sum of money. Some gladiators became so popular that people used to write graffiti about them on the walls of buildings around Rome!

249 Gladiators fought wild beasts. Animals such as lions, tigers and crocodiles were brought from distant parts of the Empire to be hunted by gladiators in the arena. Sometimes criminals with no weapons were put into the arena along with the wild animals. They did not last long.

250 The Colosseum was an amazing building for its time. Also known as the Flavian Amphitheatre, it was a huge oval arena in the centre of Rome, used for gladiator fights and the executions of criminals. It opened in AD 80, and could seat 50,000 people. It was built of stone, concrete and marble and had 80 separate entrances.

▼ The Colosseum was the largest amphitheatre in the Roman empire.

▶ Chariot drivers wore helmets, but no other protective clothing.

251 Some Romans liked a day at the races. Horses pulled fast chariots round racetracks, called 'circuses'. The most famous was the Circus Maximus in Rome, which could hold 250,000 spectators. There could be up to 24 races each day. Twelve chariots took part in each race, running seven times round the oval track – a total distance of about 8 kilometres.

252 Chariots often collided and overturned. Each charioteer carried a sharp knife, called a *falx*, to cut himself free from the wreckage. Even so, many horses and charioteers were killed.

253 Racing rivalries sometimes led to riots. Races were organized by four separate teams – the Reds, Blues, Greens and Whites. Charioteers wore tunics in their team colours. Each team had a keen – and violent – group of fans.

Ruling Rome

254 According to legend, the first king, Romulus, came to power in 753 BC. Six kings ruled after him, but they were unjust and cruel. After King Tarquin the Proud was overthrown in 509 BC Rome became a republic (a state without a king). Every year the people elected two consuls (senior lawyers) to head the government. Other officials were elected too. The republic lasted for over 400 years.

255 In 47 BC a successful general called Julius Caesar declared himself dictator. This meant that he wanted to rule on his own for life. Many people feared that he was trying to end the republic, and rule like the old kings. Caesar was murdered in 44 BC by his political enemies. After this, there were many years of civil war.

▲ Legend says the twins Romulus and Remus were suckled by a wolf before being rescued by a shepherd.

I DON'T BELIEVE IT!

Some Roman emperors were mad and even dangerous. Emperor Nero was said to have laughed and played music while watching a terrible fire that destroyed a large part of Rome.

▲ This relief shows the emperor Trajan speaking to his army in AD 106. By this date emperors would command the army in battle and were expected to be talented generals.

256
In 27 BC Caesar's nephew Octavian seized power in Rome. He declared himself 'First Citizen', and said he would bring back peace and good government to Rome. He ended the civil war, and introduced many strong new laws. But he also changed the Roman government forever. He took a new name, 'Augustus', and became the first emperor of Rome.

257
Later the army took over. In 193 Emperor Commodus was murdered and the senate met to decide who would take over. The army marched to Rome and made Septimus Severus emperor. After this it was the army who decided who would be emperor.

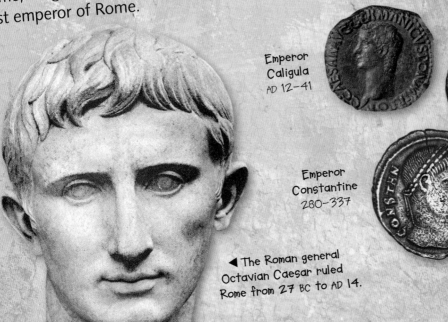

Emperor Caligula
AD 12–41

Emperor Nero
AD 37–68

Emperor Constantine
280–337

◀ The emperors put their portraits on coins to remind everyone who was in charge of the empire.

◀ The Roman general Octavian Caesar ruled Rome from 27 BC to AD 14.

In the army

258 Being a soldier was a good career, if you didn't get killed! Roman soldiers were well paid and cared for. The empire needed troops to defend its land against attack, and soldiers were well trained. Good fighters were promoted and received extra pay. When they retired they were given money or land.

259 Roman troops carried three main weapons. They fought with javelins, swords and daggers. Each man had to buy his own set, and look after them carefully – one day, his life might depend on them.

260 Soldiers needed many skills. On arrival at a new base they set up camps of tents, but soon afterwards built permanent forts defended by strong walls. Each legion contained men with a wide range of skills, such as cooks, builders, doctors, carpenters, blacksmiths and engineers – but they all had to fight!

▶ Soldiers used their shields to make a protective shell called a *testudo*, or 'tortoise'.

◀ Roman soldiers used the *gladius*, a stabbing sword about 80 centimetres long.

◄ The ballista was a weapon that could hurl a heavy javelin accurately over a range of 500 metres.

261 The army could march up to 30 kilometres in a day. When they were hurrying to put down a rebellion, or moving from fort to fort, soldiers travelled quickly, on foot. Troops marched along straight, well-made army roads. Each soldier had to carry a heavy pack containing weapons, armour, tools, cooking pots, food and spare clothes.

262 The army contained citizens and 'helpers'. Roman citizens joined the regular army. Men who were not citizens could also fight for Rome. They were known as auxiliaries (helpers) and were organized into special units of their own.

263 Roman soldiers guarding the northern frontiers of Britain had to endure cold temperatures. They kept warm by wearing short woollen trousers – like underpants – beneath their tunics.

◄ Roman cavalry were usually auxiliary troops raised from non-Roman peoples.

264 Soldiers worshipped their own special god. At forts and army camps, soldiers built temples where they honoured the god Mithras, who they believed protected them and gave them life after death.

Ruled by Rome

265 More than 50 million people were ruled by Rome. Celts, Germans, Iberians, and many other peoples lived in territories held by Rome's armies. They had their own languages, customs and beliefs. Rome sent governors to force conquered peoples to pay Roman taxes and obey Roman laws.

▼ The Roman city of Londinium (London) was built where a bridge could be built over the wide River Thames.

266 A few conquered kings and queens did not accept Roman rule. In AD 60 Boudicca, queen of the Iceni tribe of eastern England, led a rebellion against the Romans in Britain. Her army marched on London and other cities but was defeated by Roman soldiers.

▼ British warriors led by Queen Boudicca destroyed cities and killed everyone they found.

LOOK LIKE A CELTIC WARRIOR!

Roman writers reported how Celtic warriors decorated their faces and bodies with patterns before going into battle. They believed that the paint was magic, and would protect them. The Celts used a deep-blue dye made from a plant called woad. Ask an adult if you have some special face-painting make-up, then try using it to make up some scary war-paint designs of your own.

267 Cleopatra used beauty and charm to stop the Romans invading. Cleopatra was queen of Egypt and she knew that the Egyptian army would not be able to defeat Roman soldiers. Two Roman army generals, Julius Caesar and Mark Antony, fell in love with Cleopatra. She prevented the Romans invading for many years, but Egypt was eventually conquered.

▶ Queen Cleopatra shown wearing the traditional clothing of an Egyptian queen.

▼ This map shows the Roman Empire in brown, and the roads that they built in black.

268 Romans built monuments to celebrate their victories. Trajan, who ruled from AD 98–117, was a Roman soldier who became emperor. After his army conquered Dacia (now Romania) in AD 106, he gave orders for a 30-metre-high stone pillar to be built in the Forum in Rome. The pillar was decorated with carvings of 2500 Roman soldiers winning wars. It still stands today and is known as Trajan's Column.

The farming life

269 **Rome relied on farmers.** Most Romans lived in the countryside and worked on farms. Farmers produced food for city-dwellers. Food was grown on big estates by teams of slaves, and on small peasant farms where single families worked together.

270 **Farm produce was imported from all over the empire.** Wool and honey came from Britain, wine from Greece, and 400,000 tonnes of wheat were shipped across the Mediterranean Sea from Egypt every year. It was ground into flour, which was used to make bread, the Romans' basic food.

▼ A relief showing a merchant taking delivery of large pottery amphorae (tall jugs or jars) filled with oil or wine.

▲ Slaves work the land on a large Roman estate.

271 **Roman grapes grew on trees.** Vines (climbing plants that produce grapes) were planted among fruit trees in orchards. The trees provided support for the vine stems, and welcome shade to stop the grapes getting scorched by the sun. Grapes were one of the most important crops on Roman farms. The ripe fruits were picked and dried to become raisins, or pulped and made into wine.

KEY

1 Beehives for honey
2 Treading grapes for wine
3 Owner of the farm
4 Vineyard and orchard
5 Threshing wheat
6 Sheep kept in fields
7 Pressing olives
8 Farmworkers harvesting grain
9 Vegetable patch

272
The most valuable fruit was small, hard, green and bitter! Olives could be pickled in salty water to eat with bread and cheese, or crushed to provide oil. The Romans used olive oil as a medicine, for cooking and preserving food, for cleaning and softening the skin, and even for burning in lamps.

273
Farmers didn't have machines to help them. Heavy work was done by animals or humans, and ploughs were pulled by oxen. Crops were harvested by men and women using sickles (curved knives) and loaded onto carts by hand. Donkeys turned mill wheels to crush olives, grind grain, and to raise drinking water from wells.

▶ This mosaic shows dates being harvested.

TRUE OR FALSE?

1. The Romans imported wool and honey from Britain.
2. A raisin is a dried olive.
3. The Romans used olive oil as a medicine.

Answers:
1. True 2. False 3. True

Work like a slave

274 In Rome not all people were equal. How you were treated in society depended on your class. Free-born people (citizens) had rights that were guaranteed by law – for example, to travel or find work. Citizens could vote in elections, and receive free food handouts. Slaves had very few rights. They belonged to their owners just like dogs or horses.

275 From 73–71 BC a slave called Spartacus led revolt in southern Italy. He ran away to a hideout in the hills where 90,000 other slaves joined him.

276 Slaves were purchased from slave-traders or born to slave parents. People could also be condemned to slavery as a punishment for a serious crime, or if they were captured in a war.

▼ Slaves were bought and sold at slave-markets. They were paraded before the citizens to be chosen or rejected. The slaves could not leave, or choose what work to do. They could be cruelly punished, neglected or given away.

◀ Slaves at work in a Roman mosaic from about the year AD 500. They were expected to wear simple tunics.

277
Slaves were trained to do all sorts of tasks. They did everything their owners demanded, from looking after children to hard labour on farms. Many slaves were trusted by their owners, who valued their skills. A few slaves became respected chefs or doctors.

278
Sometimes slaves were set free by their owners. Freedom could be a reward for loyalty or long service. Some sick or dying slave-owners gave orders that their slaves should be freed. They did not want their slaves to pass to a new owner who might treat them badly.

279
Some slaves did very well after they were freed. Former slaves used the skills they had learned to set up businesses of their own. Many were successful, and a few became very rich.

Roman know-how

280 The Romans pioneered new building materials and designs. They discovered concrete, which was much cheaper and easier to use than stone. They baked clay at high temperatures to make long-lasting bricks. They used arches to create tall, strong walls and doorways. They designed massive domes for buildings that were too big to be roofed with wooden beams.

281 Aqueducts brought 750 million litres of fresh water to the city of Rome every day. This water was carried by pipes to public fountains and rich people's homes.

▼ The Romans were amazing builders and architects. Their roads and many of their buildings have lasted more than 2000 years.

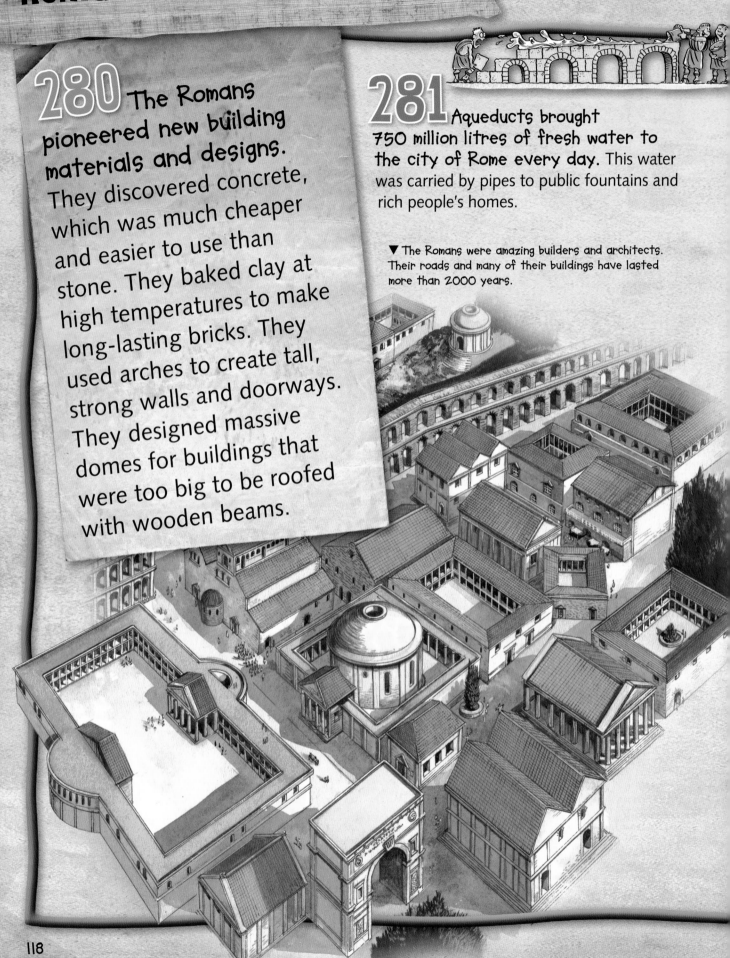

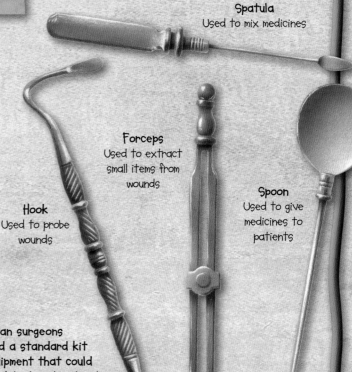

◀ Romans used valves to pump water uphill. Water would then come out of fountains.

284
Even the best doctors often failed to cure their patients. But Roman doctors were skilled at sewing up cuts and joining broken bones. They also used herbs for medicines and painkillers.

282
No one improved on the Romans' water supplies until the 1800s! They invented pumps with valves to pump water uphill. This went into high tanks above fountains. Gravity pulled the water out of the fountain's spout.

283
Despite their advanced technology, Romans believed that illness was caused by witchcraft. To find a cure, they made a special visit to a temple, to ask the gods with healing powers to make them better.

Spatula
Used to mix medicines

Forceps
Used to extract small items from wounds

Hook
Used to probe wounds

Spoon
Used to give medicines to patients

▶ Roman surgeons carried a standard kit of equipment that could be used to treat patients and deal with different types of injuries.

Prayers and sacrifices

Juno
Queen of the gods and patron of marriage

Jupiter
King of the gods and god of the sky

Minerva
Goddess of the arts and of wisdom, daughter of Jupiter

Neptune
God of rivers, the sea and earthquakes, brother of Jupiter

Mars
God of warfare and peace treaties, ancestor of the Roman people

Venus
Represented love and beauty, like the Greek goddess Aphrodite

Apollo
Greek god of arts, light and prophecy, worshipped in Rome from 430 BC

Diana
Goddess of hunting, the moon and childbirth, daughter of Jupiter

Vulcan
God of fire and blacksmiths, husband of Venus, son of Jupiter

Vesta
Goddess of home and family, her temple had an eternal flame

Mercury
God of business, money and travel, messenger of the gods

Ceres
Goddess of grain crops and farmers, sister of Jupiter

285 **The Romans had many gods.** There were gods of the city, the country, and of the underworld, and some were worshipped by people of certain professions. The Romans even adopted gods from other countries that were part of the empire. Ideas and gods from Greece had a very big impact.

286 **The emperor was also chief priest.** As part of his duties he said prayers and offered sacrifices to the gods who protected Rome. His title was *pontifex maximus* (chief bridge-builder) because people believed he acted as a bridge between the gods and ordinary people.

287 **Families made offerings to the gods every day.** They left food, wine and incense in front of a shrine in their house. A shrine is like a mini temple. It contained statues of ancient gods called the *lares* and *penates*. The *lares* were ancestor spirits who looked after living family members. The *penates* guarded the family's food.

▲ A Roman pours a libation (small offering) to the gods, onto the ground at a temple.

288 **Romans were superstitious.** They decorated their homes with magic symbols, and children were made to wear good-luck charms. They thought they could foretell the future by observing animals – bees were a sign of riches but a hooting owl foretold danger.

289 **Some of the first Christians lived in Rome.** For years Christianity was banned in Rome, so Christians met secretly in catacombs (underground passages). They also used the catacombs as burial places. The persecution of Christians ended after 313, and in 380 Christianity became the official state religion of Rome.

On the move

290 Rome was at the hub of a network of roads that stretched for more than 85,000 kilometres. It had been built to link outlying parts of the empire to the capital, so that Roman armies or government officials could travel quickly. To make travel as quick as possible, roads were built in straight lines, taking the shortest route.

▲ A street in Pompeii. The stepping stones were provided so people could cross without treading in horse droppings and rubbish.

291 Rome's first main road was built in 312 BC. Its name was the Via Appia (*via* is the Latin word for 'road'). It ran from Rome to the port of Brundisium on the south-east coast of Italy. Many travellers from Greece arrived there, and the new road made their journey to Rome quicker and easier.

292 Some Roman roads have survived for over 2000 years. Each road was made of layers of earth and stones on top of a firm, flat foundation. It was surfaced with stone slabs or gravel. The centre had a camber (curved surface), so that rainwater drained away into ditches on either side.

Large surface slabs

Drainage ditch

▶ Trained men worked out the route, and slaves did the heavy labour. Army roads were built by soldiers.

Solid foundations

Route accurately marked out

293

Engineers used special tools to help them make accurate surveys. They made careful plans and took measurements before starting any building project, such as a new road or city walls.

▼ These engineers are using a *groma* to measure straight lines on a road.

294

Poor people walked everywhere. They couldn't afford to hire a horse or donkey, or a carriage pulled by oxen. With luck they could hitch a lift in a farm wagon – but it wouldn't be a comfortable ride!

295

Town streets were crowded and dirty. Rich people travelled in curtained beds called litters, carried by slaves. Stepping stones allowed ordinary people to avoid the mud and rubbish underfoot.

296

Heavy loads often travelled by water. There were no lorries in Roman times. Ships, powered by sails and by slaves rowing, carried people and cargo over water. But water-transport was slow, and could be dangerous. Roman ships were often attacked by pirates, and shipwrecks were common.

◄ A Roman war galley. The ram at the bow could be used to sink enemy ships, or the soldiers might fight their way on board enemy ships.

Uncovering the past

297 Lots of evidence survives to tell us about Roman times. Archaeologists have discovered the remains of many Roman buildings, from palaces and aqueducts, to temples, hospitals and homes. They have also found works of art, coins, jewellery, pottery, glass, and many tools and objects used in daily life.

298 The oceans contain secrets from the past. Marine archaeology is the hunt for amazing relics under the sea. Many Roman shipwrecks have been discovered in the Mediterranean Sea, including a wine carrier with 6000 amphorae off the coast near Marseilles in France.

▼ Archaeologists find a Roman pot in the bed of the Ljubljanica River in Slovenia. Underwater techniques are relatively new and have allowed archaeologists to make dramatic discoveries.

A mosaic preserved at Herculaneum shows Roman gods.

QUIZ

1. What does the name Marcus mean?
2. Which of these things would not be discovered by an archaeologist studying ancient Rome: glass, telephone, coin?
3. What is marine archaeology?

Answers:
1. God of War 2. A telephone
3. The study of relics underwater

Roman coins have survived in large numbers allowing us to study emperors and gods.

299 Until the 20th century, grand, important buildings were often planned and decorated in Roman style. Architects believed that Roman designs inspired respect, so many cities have churches, museums, art galleries, colleges and even banks that look like Roman temples or Roman villas.

300 Roman names are still quite common. In some parts of the world, children are given Roman names or names based on Latin words. These include Amanda (Loveable), Diana (Moon Goddess), Patricia (Noble), Laura (Laurel-tree), Marcus (God of War), Victor (Winner), and Vincent (Conqueror).

▲ Casts of bodies found in Pompeii. The casts are made by pouring plaster into hollow spaces left in the volcanic ash where bodies have rotted away.

WARRIORS

301 **Warriors are people who fight in battles.** A warrior is often a soldier or trained fighter who has shown great courage. Great warriors have the power to capture our imagination. Throughout history to the present day, the cry of the warrior has been heard around the world.

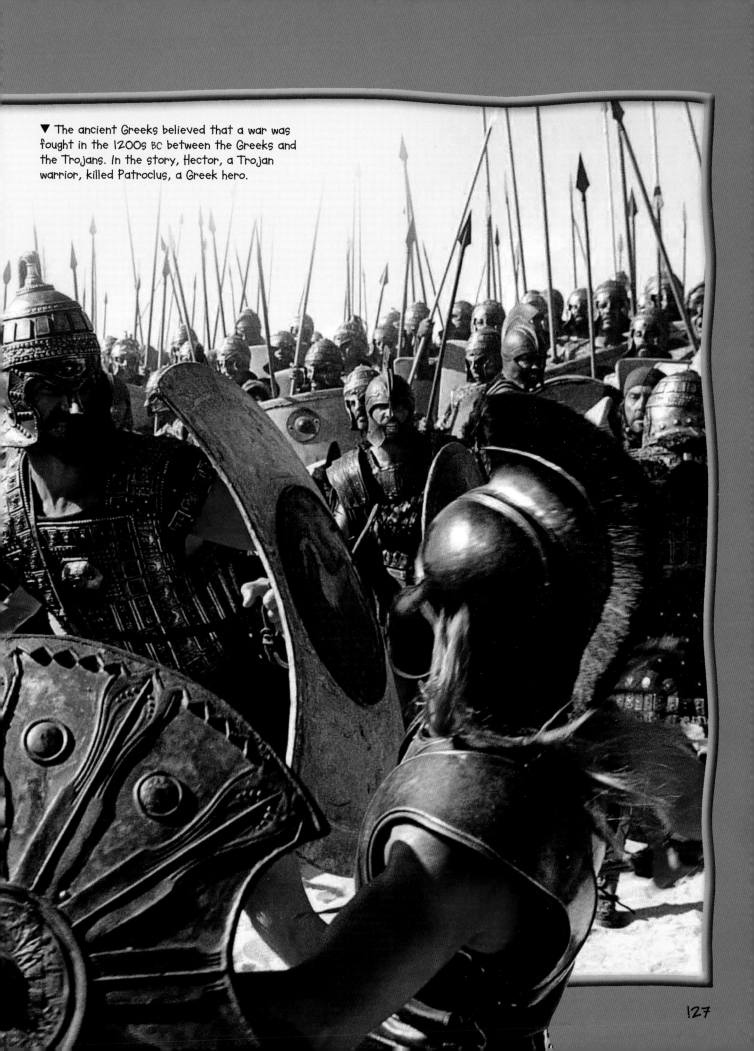

▼ The ancient Greeks believed that a war was fought in the 1200s BC between the Greeks and the Trojans. In the story, Hector, a Trojan warrior, killed Patroclus, a Greek hero.

The first warriors

302 The earliest warriors lived in prehistoric times. Archaeologists divide prehistory into three ages. First the Stone Age, when stone was used to make tools and weapons. Then the Bronze Age, when metal was first used. After this came the Iron Age, when iron took over from bronze.

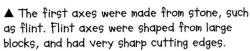

▲ The first axes were made from stone, such as flint. Flint axes were shaped from large blocks, and had very sharp cutting edges.

304 The first warriors must have been brave. A fighter may have had to prove his bravery before becoming a warrior. He could have been set challenges to test his courage, or have been made to perform tasks in a ceremony. Only by passing the tests would he have been accepted as a warrior by the rest of his group.

303 Prehistoric people used a range of weapons. Many axes, sling stones, arrows, swords and daggers survive today, but weapons made of perishable materials, such as wood, rotted away long ago. From the weapons that have survived, we can tell that prehistoric people lived in violent times.

◄ ► Weapons of prehistoric warriors – a spear, an axe and a sword.

Iron sword

Stone spear

Bronze axe

QUIZ

1. What are the three ages of prehistory?
2. Which metal took over from bronze?
3. How many arrowheads were found at Crickley Hill?

Answers:
1. Stone Age, Bronze Age, Iron Age
2. Iron 3. More than 400

PREHISTORIC TIMELINE

The division of prehistory into three main ages is based on the technology of each period.

1,000,000–8500 BC	8500–7000 BC	7000–2750 BC	2750–750 BC	750–50 BC
Palaeolithic or Old Stone Age	Mesolithic or Middle Stone Age	Neolithic or New Stone Age	Bronze Age	Iron Age

305 Prehistoric battles were fought for many reasons. Rivalries between groups might have been a good reason to go to war, so arguments over who owned land and other property may have led to battles. If different people in a group wanted to be the leader, the only way to decide may have been to fight it out.

306 An arrow battle was fought in prehistoric times at Crickley Hill, in Gloucestershire, England. On top of the hill is a Neolithic (New Stone Age) camp. Archaeologists found more than 400 flint arrowheads scattered around the two entrances to the camp. It seems the camp was the site of a full-scale arrow battle, about 4500 years ago.

▶ A prehistoric hunting party equipped with bows and spears.

Warriors of Mesopotamia

307 The first armies were in Mesopotamia – a region of the Middle East where present-day Iran and Iraq are found. Here, men were first organized into fighting forces around 4500 years ago. Kings wanted to show power, and controlling an army was a way to do this. King Sargon (2334–2279 BC) was the first Mesopotamian ruler to have a full-time army.

▲ Mesopotamia was an area of the Middle East between the rivers Euphrates and Tigris.

I DON'T BELIEVE IT!

Using a composite bow, a Mesopotamian archer could fire an arrow up to about 245 metres.

308 Mesopotamian armies had hundreds of thousands of troops. They were organized into foot soldiers (infantry), horse soldiers (cavalry) and the most feared of all – charioteers. Chariots were wheeled, horse-drawn platforms used for archers to shoot from. Some battles involved hundreds of chariots.

▲ Mounted archers were a rapid strike force of Assyrian armies. Assyria was a kingdom of northern Mesopotamia.

310 The Battle of Carchemish was fought in 605 BC. The battle was between the Babylonians (one of the peoples of Mesopotamia) and the ancient Egyptians. The Babylonian army destroyed the Egyptian army, and the surviving Egyptian forces fled. The Babylonians gave chase, and a second battle took place near the Sea of Galilee, in Palestine. The Egyptians were defeated again, and retreated into Egypt.

311 Mesopotamian myths tell of warrior heroes. The greatest was Gilgamesh who, according to legend, defeated evil monsters. On a quest for immortality (eternal life), Gilgamesh was set a test to stay awake for seven nights. But he fell asleep, failing the test, and so never became immortal.

▶ In the legend of Gilgamesh, the warrior killed a hideous giant called Humbaba.

309 The Mesopotamian warrior's main weapon was the bow. At first, bows were made from single pieces of wood, but then people discovered how to make bows from layers of wood and bone glued together. These were called composite bows, and they fired arrows further than one-piece bows.

Alexander

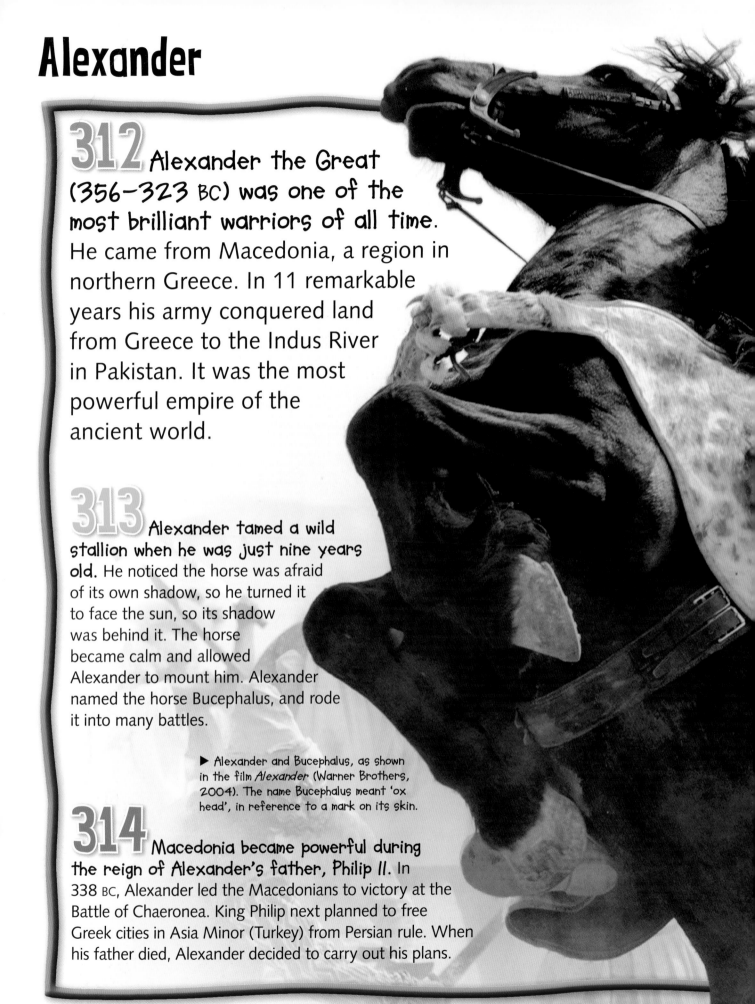

312 Alexander the Great (356–323 BC) was one of the most brilliant warriors of all time. He came from Macedonia, a region in northern Greece. In 11 remarkable years his army conquered land from Greece to the Indus River in Pakistan. It was the most powerful empire of the ancient world.

313 Alexander tamed a wild stallion when he was just nine years old. He noticed the horse was afraid of its own shadow, so he turned it to face the sun, so its shadow was behind it. The horse became calm and allowed Alexander to mount him. Alexander named the horse Bucephalus, and rode it into many battles.

▶ Alexander and Bucephalus, as shown in the film *Alexander* (Warner Brothers, 2004). The name Bucephalus meant 'ox head', in reference to a mark on its skin.

314 Macedonia became powerful during the reign of Alexander's father, Philip II. In 338 BC, Alexander led the Macedonians to victory at the Battle of Chaeronea. King Philip next planned to free Greek cities in Asia Minor (Turkey) from Persian rule. When his father died, Alexander decided to carry out his plans.

315
Alexander raised an army of 43,000 hoplites and 5500 cavalry. Soon after entering the Persian Empire, Alexander's army defeated a Persian army at the Battle of the Granicus River (334 BC). This opened the way to the Greek cities of Asia Minor, which Alexander freed from Persian control.

▶ The Battle of the Granicus River was fought in present-day Turkey.

316
Alexander's greatest battle against the Persians was the Battle of Issus in 333 BC. His army of 35,000 troops met the army of Darius III, king of Persia, at Issus, in modern-day southern Turkey. Alexander's army was victorious, despite being outnumbered two to one. Later that year he defeated the Persians at the Battle of Gaugamela (in present-day Iraq). Then Alexander led his army into the heart of the Persian Empire, taking city after city.

▶ A mosaic of the Battle of Issus, showing Darius III and his army.

I DON'T BELIEVE IT!
Alexander the Great marched a massive total of around 32,000 kilometres over the course of his 11-year battle campaign.

Boudicca

I DON'T BELIEVE IT!

Underneath Colchester, London and St Albans, there is still a thick layer of burnt earth, left from Boudicca's attacks on them.

317 **Boudicca was a warrior queen.** She was from a Celtic tribe called the Iceni, which lived in the east of Britain. A Roman writer described Boudicca as tall, with long red hair, and wearing a large gold necklace. Boudicca is famous for leading an uprising against the Romans.

318 **Boudicca's husband, King Prasutagus, died around AD 60.** He left half his kingdom to the Romans and the other half to Boudicca. The Romans wanted all of it, and set about taking it by force. So during AD 60 and AD 61, Boudicca led the Iceni and other British tribes in a rebellion against the Romans.

▶ Boudicca, warrior queen of the Iceni, fought the Romans in Britain.

319 **Boudicca is said to have led more than 100,000 warriors against the Romans.** Known as the Britons, they fought with swords and spears, and protected themselves with shields. Some rode into battle in chariots. They were brave warriors, but were not as organized as the Romans.

320

Boudicca's warriors went south to fight, to the Roman towns of south-east Britain. They burned the towns of Camulodunum (Colchester), Londinium (London) and Verulamium (St Albans), killing some 70,000 civilians and destroying the Roman IXth Legion.

321

Boudicca's last battle was somewhere in the English Midlands. As many as 230,000 Britons fought a smaller Roman force. However, the Romans had better tactics and weapons, and 80,000 Britons are said to have died. The Romans won, and Boudicca died soon after, possibly by ending her own life with poison.

Norman warriors

322 In AD 911, a Viking warband led by Rollo arrived in northern France. At first the region was known as *Nordmannia* ('Northman's Land'). The Vikings settled in the area and it became known as Normandy. The warriors who came from this area were the Normans.

▲ In 1066, the Normans departed from St Valery in northern France and landed at Pevensey in southern England, ready to do battle.

323 The Normans were skilled fighters, organizers and builders. In the AD 1000s Norman armies conquered England, much of France, southern Italy and Sicily. They also took part in the Crusades to the Holy Land (Palestine).

324 A Norman army was made up of many foot soldiers. They fought with spears, axes and bows. The cavalry was the strongest part of the army. Cavalry soldiers owned their own horses and went to war in the hope of being rewarded for their service.

325
In battle, Norman foot soldiers formed themselves into defensive shield walls or war hedges. The front ranks held their long shields close together, forming a solid barrier that protected the warriors behind it from missiles. The shield wall came apart to allow the fighters to use their weapons, and for the cavalry to charge through.

326
On 28 September, 1066, William, Duke of Normandy, invaded England. He led about 750 ships across the English Channel from France. Onboard was an army of 10,000 men and 3000 horses. On 14 October, 1066, the Normans defeated the English in the Battle of Hastings. Harold, the king of England, was killed, and William became the first Norman king of England. He was known as William the Conqueror.

◄ At Senlac Hill, near Hastings, Norman soldiers charged uphill to attack the English.

QUIZ
1. What area of France did the Normans come from?
2. What was the strongest part of a Norman army?
3. In what year was the Battle of Hastings?

Answers:
1. Normandy
2. The cavalry 3. 1066

Saladin

327 Saladin (1137–1193) was a Muslim warrior. He led a religious war (*jihad*) in the Middle East. Saladin (or Salah ad-Din Yuseuf) became a soldier at 14, and for many years fought against other Muslims in Egypt. By 1187, he had become the sultan (ruler) of Egypt and Syria, and decided to drive Christians out of the holy city of Jerusalem.

▲ Both sides used mounted troops in their battles.

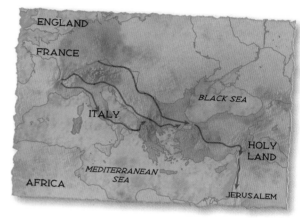

▲ Routes taken by Crusader armies as they travelled to the Holy Land.

328 The Battle of Hattin was fought in July 1187. It was a major battle between Muslims, led by Saladin, and Christians, led by Guy of Lusignan, and took place near Lake Tiberias in northern Palestine. Guy had about 20,000 troops, but Saladin's army was half as big again. Perhaps as few as 3000 Christian warriors survived the battle. It was an important victory for Saladin.

◄ Muslim warriors were lightly armoured and fought with curved swords.

329 The series of religious wars fought in the Holy Land (Palestine) between Muslims and Christians were called Crusades. Between 1096 and 1291, Christian soldiers travelled from Europe to the Holy Land, where they fought to curb the spread of Islam, retake Jerusalem, and protect Christian pilgrims who went there.

330 After the Battle of Hattin, Saladin conquered Christian strongholds in the Holy Land. He took Acre and Jaffa in present-day Israel, and Beirut in Lebanon. By September 1187 his army had reached Jerusalem. The Christians surrendered after a short siege. Saladin showed some mercy, allowing some Christians to leave the city in return for a ransom. The rest he sold into slavery.

331 Saladin's warriors were mostly lightly armed mounted archers. They wore little body armour, so they could ride much faster than their Christian foes who wore heavy metal armour. Speed was the Muslim warriors' secret of success. They preferred to engage in skirmishes, picking off their enemies with well-aimed arrows before making their escape. This way, they weakened their opponents.

▶ The forces of Saladin's army besiege the city of Jerusalem in 1187, as shown in the film *Kingdom of Heaven* (Twentieth Century Fox, 2005).

Richard the Lionheart

332 King Richard I (1157–1199) was king of England for ten years, from 1189 to 1199. He was known as *Coeur de Lion*, or Richard the Lionheart, because of his success as a military leader and warrior.

▶ King Richard I led an army of crusaders to the Holy Land.

333 Richard, the Holy Roman Emperor Frederick I (king of Germany and Italy), and King Philip II of France organized a crusade to free Jerusalem from Saladin. This was the Third Crusade, and lasted from 1189 to 1192. On reaching the Holy Land, the first action of Richard's knights was to capture the city of Acre from the Muslims. They did this in July 1191, with the use of battering rams and catapults.

334 After taking Acre, Richard marched towards Jerusalem. His progress was stopped in September 1191, when he fought Saladin at the Battle of Arsuf. The Christian and Muslim armies each had about 20,000 warriors, and although the battle was a victory for Richard, Saladin's army was able to regroup and continue with its hit-and-run skirmishes.

▼ King Richard's army besieged the city of Acre for about six weeks.

Trebuchet

Siege tower

Catapult

Battering ram

335 Richard came to within about 19 kilometres of Jerusalem. He was unable to attack it as his supplies were low and Saladin's constant skirmishes had picked off too many of his troops. The two leaders made peace, and in return for Richard agreeing to leave, Saladin allowed Christian pilgrims to visit Jerusalem, ending the Third Crusade.

336 The crusaders set sail for home, but Richard's adventures weren't over. While travelling overland from Venice, he was captured by an Austrian enemy, and handed over to Henry VI of Germany. A ransom of 150,000 silver marks (a unit of currency) was demanded for his release. After being held for over a year, the ransom was paid, and Richard returned home.

Warrior monks

337 Crusader armies were composed of foot soldiers and mounted knights. Among the knights were warriors who belonged to religious groups or orders. They followed strict rules, and were organized in a similar way to monks in monasteries. These 'warrior monks' were anything but peaceful.

DESIGN A SHIELD

Medieval knights carried shields made of wood and covered with coloured leather. They had pictures or patterns (coats of arms) on them so knights could recognize their friends in battle. Look for pictures of shields in books or on the Internet. Then have a go at drawing and colouring a design of your own.

338 The Knights Hospitaller were founded in Jerusalem in 1099. At first their role was to provide safe lodgings for Christian pilgrims to the city, and to care for the sick and wounded in their hospital. This gradually became a sizeable military force, acting as armed guards for pilgrims and crusaders. The Knights Hospitaller were also known as the Knights of St John.

▶ The symbol of the Knights Templar – two knights on one horse.

339 The Knights Templar were founded in Jerusalem in 1119 by nine French knights. They were called Templars because their headquarters were on the site of the Temple of Solomon. The Knights Templar were the most disciplined and bravest crusaders. They were also the richest, thanks to donations from Christians in Europe.

340 **The German Teutonic Knights were founded at Acre in 1198.** They were formed to protect Christian pilgrims, but took up arms against Muslims and built castles. Active in the Holy Land until the 1290s, their main work was carried out later in the Baltic region, fighting in Lithuania.

◀ Knights took part in jousting tournaments, charging at each other with lances.

341 **The armoured knight was the elite warrior of medieval Europe.** In childhood he was taught to ride and to use a sword and lance. As a knight, he took part in tournaments to improve his fighting skills, ready for when he went to war.

▶ Knights marched with colourful pennants (triangular flags).

Genghis Khan

342 Mongol warrior Genghis Khan (1162–1227) ruled with great discipline. He was born in Mongolia, and given the name Temujin. The Mongols were one of many tribes that lived on the grassy plains (steppe) of central Asia. They were horsemen who followed their herds of animals.

▲ Genghis Khan was a fearless warrior who led his Mongol troops to victory.

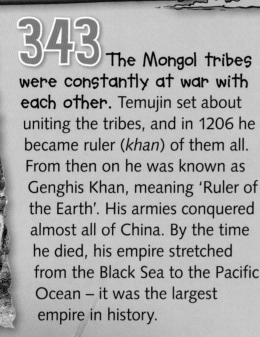

343
The Mongol tribes were constantly at war with each other. Temujin set about uniting the tribes, and in 1206 he became ruler (*khan*) of them all. From then on he was known as Genghis Khan, meaning 'Ruler of the Earth'. His armies conquered almost all of China. By the time he died, his empire stretched from the Black Sea to the Pacific Ocean – it was the largest empire in history.

344
Mongol warriors wore leather armour and helmets, and fired arrows from powerful bows as they rode. Soldiers also carried swords, maces, axes and sometimes short spears with hooks on their points. Mongol warriors each had a string of horses, and changed their mounts often, so as not to tire them.

▶ The Mongol Empire covered much of Asia and beyond.

345
Mongol warriors were organized into large groups, which were divided into units of ten (an *arban*). In battle, they would pretend to flee to make their enemy give chase. When the pursuing troops became disorganized the Mongols would turn on them, closing in to trap them.

346
The Battle of the Indus River was fought in 1221, in present-day Pakistan. A Mongol army of 10,000 faced Muslim troops of 5000 on the banks of the river. The Mongols inflicted heavy losses, and only a few Muslim soldiers crossed the river to safety.

◀ Mongol cavalrymen were expert archers. Some arrows they used made whistling noises and were used to send signals.

Joan of Arc

347 Born in France, Joan of Arc (1412–1431) lived at a time when large parts of France were controlled by the English. When Joan was about 12, she believed she had a vision in which the patron saints of France commanded her to dress as a man and lead the fight to rid France of the English.

▲ France, showing the area controlled by the English.

▼ Joan of Arc was easy to spot on the battlefield because she wore a suit of white armour.

348 Joan lived during the Hundred Years' War. This was a series of wars between England and France that began in 1337. The wars were fought over English claims to be the rulers of France. Joan went to see France's *Dauphin* (crown prince), who was soon to become King Charles VII, and told him of her vision.

349 Charles gave Joan permission to travel to the city of Orléans with a French army. The city was under siege from the English. The army arrived in April 1429. Joan was dressed as a knight, and carried a banner. Within a week, the English retreated. From then on, Joan was known as the 'Maid of Orléans'.

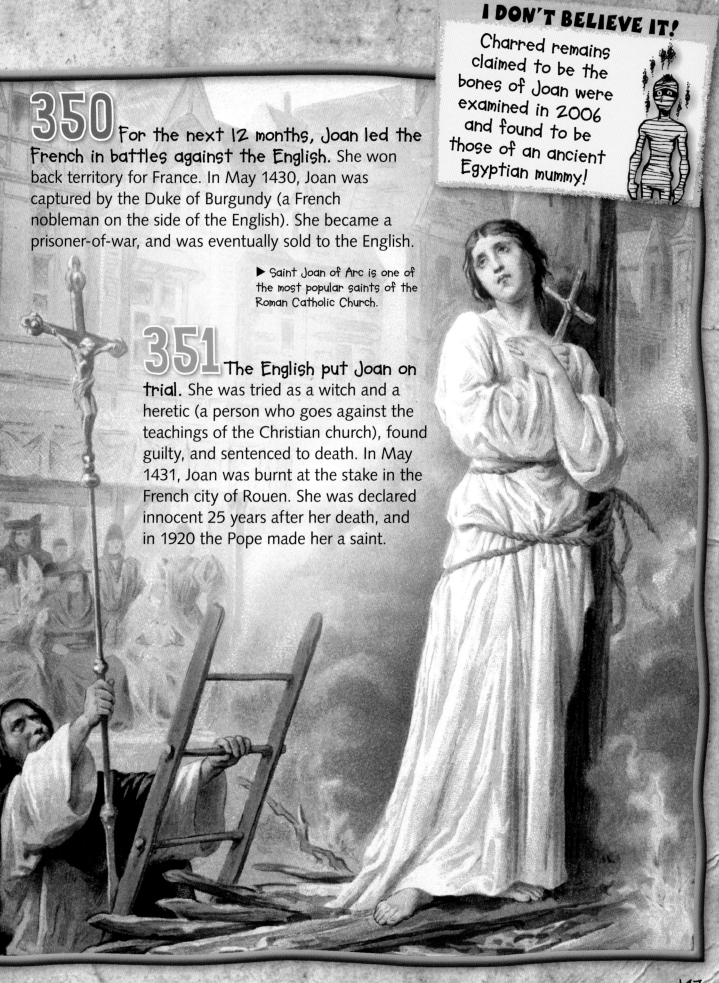

350 For the next 12 months, Joan led the French in battles against the English. She won back territory for France. In May 1430, Joan was captured by the Duke of Burgundy (a French nobleman on the side of the English). She became a prisoner-of-war, and was eventually sold to the English.

▶ Saint Joan of Arc is one of the most popular saints of the Roman Catholic Church.

351 The English put Joan on trial. She was tried as a witch and a heretic (a person who goes against the teachings of the Christian church), found guilty, and sentenced to death. In May 1431, Joan was burnt at the stake in the French city of Rouen. She was declared innocent 25 years after her death, and in 1920 the Pope made her a saint.

Moctezuma

352 The Aztecs lived in the present-day country of Mexico. They were fierce warriors who defeated rival tribes to become the strongest group in the region. The last Aztec emperor was called Moctezuma II (c. 1480–1520). He became leader of the Aztecs in 1502. He was a powerful and ruthless leader who was feared and admired by his people.

▲ Moctezuma was regarded as a god by the Aztec people.

353 The Aztecs were warriors. Every able-bodied man was expected to fight in Moctezuma's army. They were taught to use weapons as children, and at 15 they were old enough to go to war. It was considered an honour to fight for the emperor. Warriors who did well were rewarded with gifts of land and slaves.

354 The fiercest Aztec fighters were the Eagle and Jaguar warriors. Eagle warriors wore suits made from feathers, and the Jaguars dressed in ocelot skins. They were full-time soldiers, while most of the army were part-time soldiers who returned to regular jobs after the fighting was over.

355
Warriors fought with slings, bows and spears launched from spear-throwers. The most dangerous Aztec weapon was the war-club, the edges of which were covered with blades of razor-sharp obsidian (a glass-like stone made inside volcanoes). It could slice an enemy's head off in one blow.

▼ The Aztecs outnumbered the Spaniards, but the Spaniards had much better weapons.

356
In 1519, an army of Spaniards landed in Mexico in search of gold. When the news reached Moctezuma, he thought they were gods and sent them gifts, and when they first arrived in the Aztec capital he treated them as guests. He soon realized his mistake. Fighting between the Aztecs and the Spaniards began in May 1520. Moctezuma was killed, and the Aztec city was looted and destroyed.

Babur

357 The founder of the Mughal Empire in northern India was known as Babur (1483–1531). His real name was Zahir ud-Din Muhammad, but as he rose to power he was given the nickname Babur, meaning 'tiger'. He was a powerful Muslim leader.

▲ The Battle of Khanwa (1527) gave Babur control of northern India.

◄ The extent of the Mughal Empire in India.

360 In the Battle of Panipat, Babur's warriors used gunpowder weapons called arquebuses. They were an early type of bullet-firing gun, and were the most up-to-date weapons of the time. The traditional weapons of Mughal warriors were a sword with a curved blade (*talwar*) and a mace. They wore chainmail armour and carried a small round shield (*dahl*).

358 In 1504, Babur and a group of Muslim fighters captured Kabul, in Afghanistan. He established a small kingdom there, and began making raids into northern India. In 1525, he was asked to attack Ibrahim Lodi, the sultan (ruler) of Delhi, so Babur mounted a full-scale invasion of northern India.

359 Babur and Lodi's armies met at Panipat, India, in 1526. Babur had 25,000 troops, Lodi had 40,000. Lodi struck first, but failed to break through Babur's line of 700 carts tied together. After defeating Lodi's army, Babur marched to Delhi, which became the capital of the Mughal empire.

▼► Weapons of Babur's Mughal warriors.

Mace

Knife

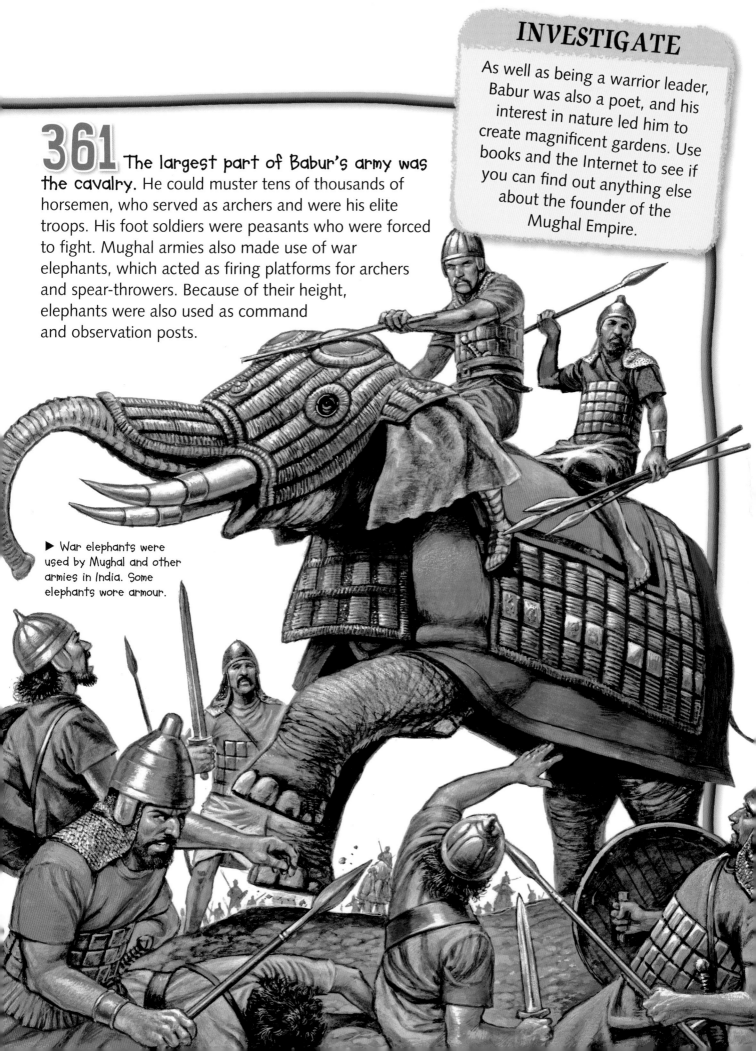

361 **The largest part of Babur's army was the cavalry.** He could muster tens of thousands of horsemen, who served as archers and were his elite troops. His foot soldiers were peasants who were forced to fight. Mughal armies also made use of war elephants, which acted as firing platforms for archers and spear-throwers. Because of their height, elephants were also used as command and observation posts.

▶ War elephants were used by Mughal and other armies in India. Some elephants wore armour.

INVESTIGATE

As well as being a warrior leader, Babur was also a poet, and his interest in nature led him to create magnificent gardens. Use books and the Internet to see if you can find out anything else about the founder of the Mughal Empire.

Napoleon Bonaparte

362 French general Napoleon Bonaparte (1769–1821) trained as a soldier from the age of ten. At 27 he was in charge of the French army in Italy. For a short time, he ruled a large part of Europe, creating the largest empire in Europe since the time of the Romans.

◀ Napoleon Bonaparte was a military genius, and one of the world's great generals.

363 Napoleon fought by new rules. He marched his army at night, attacked in the rain and on Sundays, and ordered his troops to attack the enemy at their weakest point. He was young, ambitious and ruthless. In 1799 he overthrew the government of France, and became the country's new leader. In 1804 he organized his own coronation and became Emperor Napoleon.

▼ The Battle of Austerlitz. After his victory, Napoleon said to his troops: "Soldiers! I am pleased with you!"

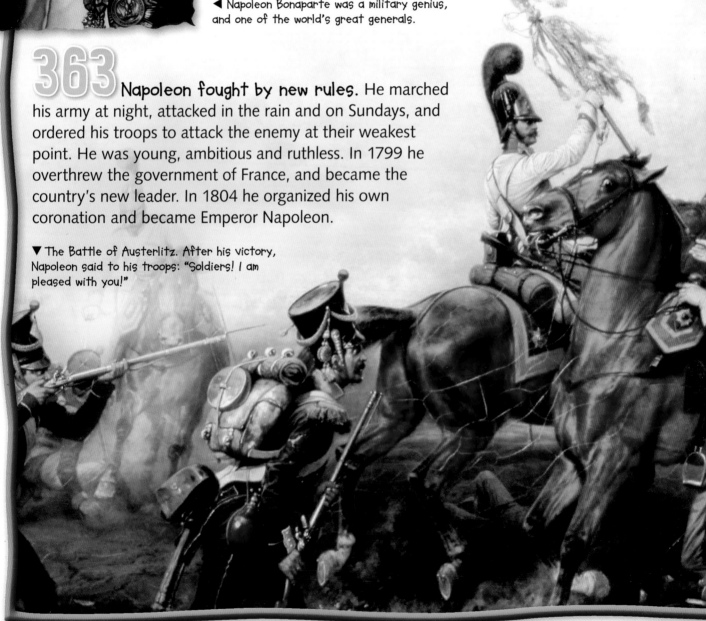

▲ The extent of Napoleon's French Empire across Europe.

364
Napoleon's greatest victory was the Battle of Austerlitz. It was fought on 2 December, 1805, in the present-day Czech Republic. Napoleon had 70,000 troops. They faced a combined army of 80,000 Russians and Austrians. The victory was a turning point for Napoleon, who sensed he could be master of all Europe.

365
In 1812, Napoleon set his sights on Russia. He invaded with an army of half a million men, and the Russians retreated. He reached Moscow, but the Russians refused to make peace. Far from home, and with supplies running low, Napoleon had no choice but to retreat. It was a bitterly cold winter, and thousands of soldiers froze to death on the march home.

366
In 1814, Austria, Russia, Prussia and Britain attacked France. They reached Paris, and Napoleon was banished to the island of Elba in the Mediterranean. He escaped and returned to France to gather a new army. His last battle was at Waterloo, on 18 June, 1815. He was defeated by an army of British and Prussians and sent to the island of St Helena in the Atlantic Ocean, where he died six years later.

I DON'T BELIEVE IT!
Napoleon was supposed to be crowned by the Pope, but when his coronation took place, Napoleon crowned himself instead.

Shaka

367 The first great chief of the Zulu nation in southern Africa was a warrior chieftain called Shaka (c. 1788–1828). He organized the army into regiments and gave his soldiers better weapons. Shaka made the Zulu nation the strongest in southern Africa.

368 Before Shaka, the Zulu people were relatively peaceful. Battles were often wars of words. Shaka changed all this, bringing in stabbing spears and training his warriors to destroy their enemies. He organized campaigns against neighbouring peoples, whom the Zulu either killed or forced to surrender.

369 Zulu boys practised fighting with sticks. At 18 they joined a regiment (*iButho*). Zulu warriors would sometimes fight duels with each other, swinging *iWisa* (clubs). It was seen as a way of making them tougher. In battle, they also used stabbing spears (*iklwa*), and throwing spears (*assegais*), and protected themselves with shields of cowhide.

▲ Shaka, the Zulu warrior chieftain. In the 1820s he ruled more than 50,000 people.

370 Zulu regiments came together in a 'buffalo horns' formation. New warriors formed the horns, experienced warriors made up the chest at the centre, and older fighters formed the body at the back. When they came within range, they threw their *assegais*. At close range, they used their stabbing spears.

371 Shaka was murdered in 1828, but the Zulu fighting spirit lived on. In 1879, the Zulu army fought the British in the Battle of Isandhlwana. The British had better weapons (rifles and bayonets), but the Zulu had more men, and they won a great victory.

▼ The British army was defeated by Zulus in the Battle of Isandhlwana (1879).

QUIZ

1. What did Zulu boys practise fighting with?
2. What were Zulu clubs called?
3. What was the Zulu battle formation called?

Answers:
1. Sticks 2. iWisa 3. Buffalo horns

Crazy Horse

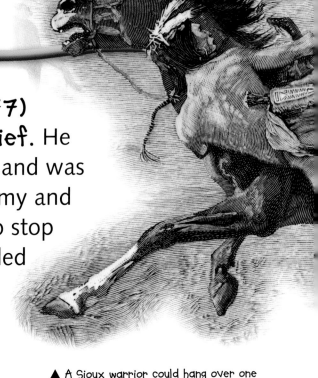

372 Crazy Horse (c. 1840–1877) was a Native American warrior chief. He belonged to the Oglala Sioux people and was involved in a struggle with the US Army and white settlers. Crazy Horse wanted to stop them taking the Sioux land, and this led to a series of battles. He said he was 'hostile to the white man' and that the Sioux wanted 'peace and to be left alone'.

▲ A Sioux warrior could hang over one side of a galloping horse, using its body as a shield against the enemy.

◀ Crazy Horse was one of the greatest of all Native American war leaders.

373 The traditional weapons of Sioux warriors were bows, lances and knives. When they came into contact with white settlers, they began trading for rifles and pistols. However, weapons were not their most prized possessions – horses were. The Sioux used horses for hunting and for war. Their horses were small and very fast, and the Sioux were expert riders.

QUIZ

1. Which Native American tribe did Crazy Horse belong to?
2. What was a Sioux warrior's most prized possession?
3. In what year was the Battle of Little Bighorn?

Answers:
1. The Sioux
2. His horse 3. 1876

375 From 1874, white settlers began moving into the Black Hills region of South Dakota, looking for gold. This was the ancestral homeland of the Sioux. The US government ordered the Sioux to leave the area, but many refused to go. Crazy Horse called for Sioux warriors to fight, and they were joined by allies from the Cheyenne and Arapaho nations.

374 As land was lost to white settlers, the Sioux began to act. Warbands of warriors began to make hit-and-run raids against US Army outposts and isolated settlements. Stagecoaches and wagon trains carrying supplies were ambushed, and telegraph wires were cut. The US Army found these tactics very difficult to fight. It was as if the Sioux were an invisible enemy.

376 The US Army was sent to clear the area of Native Americans. Crazy Horse and other leaders brought more than 1000 warriors together to resist them. On 25 and 26 June, 1876, the Battle of the Little Bighorn was fought near the Little Bighorn River, Montana. A force of 700 soldiers of the US Seventh Cavalry, led by General George Custer, was wiped out. Custer and a group of his men fought to the last on a small hill.

▼ The Battle of the Little Bighorn is also known as Custer's Last Stand.

Index

Entries in **bold** refer to main subject entries. Entries in *italics* refer to illustrations

Acknowledgements

The publishers would like to thank the following sources for the use of their photographs:
Key: t = top, b = bottom, l = left, r = right, c = centre, bg = background, rt = repeated throughout

Front cover illustration Stuart Jackson-Carter **Spine** (t) Laurence Gough/Shutterstock.com **Back cover** (l) ivan bastien/Shutterstock.com, (br) ESB Professional/Shutterstock.com

Alamy 28 Miguel Cuenca; 57 Charles Stirling (Diving); 82–83(bg) mauritius images GmbH; 88(b) Caro; 94(cr) The Art Archive; 101(tr) Artokoloro Quint Lox Limited; 128(bc) Jim Cole/Alamy; 133(tr) North Wind Picture Archives; 144–145(c) North Wind Picture Archives/Alamy Stock Photo; 156–157 North Wind Picture Archives

Dover 100–101(tc)

Fotolia.com 9 Konstantin Sutyagin; 133(br) Alfio Ferlito

Getty Images 23 Print Collector/Hulton Archive; 79(t) Richard Cummins/Corbis Documentary; 86–87(bg) Vanni Archive/Corbis Documentary; 90(t) DeA Picture Library/De Agostini Editorial; 100(bl) Roger Wood/Corbis Historical; 108(bl) DEA/G. DAGLI ORTI/De Agostini Editorial; 109(tr) Farrell Grehan; 120(t) Araldo de Luca/Corbis Collection; 121(c) Richard Baker/Corbis Historical; 124(b) Arne Hodalic/Corbis Historical; 125(b) Roger Ressmeyer/Corbis/VCG/ Corbis Documentary; 144(bg) Barry Lewis; 146(l) GraphicaArtis; 152–153(bg) Heritage Images; 154–155(bg) Rajesh Jantilal; 156(bl) Bettmann

Glow Images 40(b) SuperStock

iStockphoto.com 148(tr) Constance McGuire; 152(tl) Hulton Archive

Movie Store Collection 126–127 Warner Bros. Pictures/Helena Productions/Latina Pictures; 139(c) Twentieth Century-Fox Corporation/Scott Free Productions

National Geographic Creative 30–31(b); 36–37; 41

Rex Features 67(bl) Patrick Frilet; 81 KPA/Zuma

Science Photo Library 18–19 Henning Dalhoff

Shutterstock.com (endpapers) Luba V Nel; 2–3 Gurgen Bakhshetyan; 4–5 WDG Photo; 5(tl) leoks; 9 ChameleonsEye; 10(bg) diversepixel; 10–11(b) leoks; 14–15(bg) diversepixel; 16–17(bg) mountainpix; 34–35(bg) Luisa Fumi; 42(b) Architecteur; 42–43(bg) Eugene Sergeev; 43(b) Vladimir Korostyshevskiy; 44–45 WitR; 86(heading panel rt) Anelina, (fact panel rt) PaulPaladin; 86–87(label panels) Pakhnyushcha; 87(caption panel) David M. Schrader; 88(heading panel rt) Konstanttin; 88–89(bg) Vitaly Korovin; 89(fact panel) Apostrophe, (b)Filip Fuxa; 90(heading panel) haveseen, (caption panel rt) Valentin Agapov; 90–91(bg) Luba V Nel; 93 Ariy, (fact panel cl) Jaywarren79, (b+bg rt) Ev Thomas; 94(heading panel rt) aopsan; 94–95(panel bgs) Vitaly Korovin, (tc) Yulia Davidovich, (tr) Dionisvera; 95(herbs & spices, clockwise from tl) Noraluca013, Imageman, Robyn Mackenzie, Madlen, Volosina, (vegetables, clockwise from tl) Vladyslav Danilin, Valentyn Volkov, Dulce Rubia, Jiang Hongyan, Madlen, eye-blink, (cr) picturepartners; 96–97(bg) Tischenko Irina, (br) James Steidl, (b) Bill McKelvie; 97(c, rt) Lora liu; 98(heading panel) Valentin Agapov; 98–99(bg rt) Andre Viegas; 102(t); 102–103(bg) mg1408; 103(tr) Viacheslav Lopatin; 106(heading panel rt) Vitaly Korovin; 107(t panel) ImageState, (tr) Iakov Kalinin; 108(l panel) donatas1205; 109(br, top to bottom) Paul Picone, Chris Hill, I. Pilon, (tr panel) Molodec; 110–111(bg) Javier Rosano; 112 Piotr Zajc; 114–115(bg) javarman; 116–117(bg) RoyStudio.eu; 120(panel t) bomg, (panel c) Clipart deSIGN; 120–121(bg) donatas1205; 122 JeniFoto, 124–125 khd; 125(r) jps

Superstock 67(tr) DeAgostini; 91 imagebroker.net; 95 DeAgostini; 105(br) Album/Prisma/Album; 108–109(t) Universal Images Group; 113 and 114 DeAgostini; 115 J.D. Dallet/age fotostock; 117 Image Asset Management Ltd.; 119 Robert Harding Picture Library

TopFoto 25(t); 26(t); 99(cr); 105(bl) and 109(bl) The Granger Collection; 43(t) 2005; 54 2004 Topham Picturepoint; 62–63; 98–99(tc) AAAC; 132–133(bg) Warner Bros. Pictures/Intermedia Films/Pacifica; 147(c) Topfoto/HIP; 149(b) Topham Picturepoint; 150(tr) British Library Board; 155(tl) The Granger Collection

All other photographs are from: DigitalSTOCK, digitalvision, John Foxx, PhotoAlto, PhotoDisc, PhotoEssentials, PhotoPro, Stockbyte

All artworks are from the Miles Kelly Artwork Bank

Every effort has been made to acknowledge the source and copyright holder of each picture.
Miles Kelly Publishing apologizes for any unintentional errors or omissions.